Zoo Paradise

Zoo Paradise!

A New Model for
Humane Zoological Gardens

This way to
Zoo Paradise!

Jaime Jackson

Author, *Paddock Paradise: A Guide to Natural Horse Boarding*

Natural World Publications

Designed by Jaime Jackson.

ISBN 978-0-9997305-8-4

The reader may direct inquiries to the author at:
Jaime Jackson
P.O. Box 1765
Harrison, AR 72602-1765

Or: jacksonaanhcp@gmail.com

Table of Contents

The standard by which a zoo animal is judged
should be according to the life he lives in the wild.
— Heini Hediger ("Father of Zoo Biology")

Preface   LIKE MANY OTHERS, for years I've known that wild animals living in zoos have suffered from lives of isolation, living in close confinement, eating unnatural diets and having absolutely nothing to do — except endure the constant noise of gawking humans and zoo technology (tractors, tours buses, groundskeepers, food concessions, bitch barkers, and so forth). I've also become aware of the suffering of animals living in the wild as humans increasingly encroach upon their lives and habitats with wars, sport hunting, burgeoning suburban housing tracts and expanding cities, farming and ranching operations, roads and highways, tourism, poaching, and a growing, plundering, and insatiable corporate appetitive for all of the earth's natural resources. The very resources wildlife need if they are to survive as native species on this planet.

For many, this growing debacle has proven to be catastrophic, including complete eradication of habitat and the looming threat of extinction. Elephants, for example, numbering as many as 3

million in the late 1970s have declined to fewer than 450,000 today[1] — a downward spiral that has put regional populations on "vulnerable" to "endangered" species lists. To their credit, many countries have passed laws to protect wildlife, but turning the tide of human pressure for many species seems insurmountable and tenuous at best.

Many wild animals are now finding refuge from certain extinction in zoos, whose keepers and supporters have truly risen up to help in the highest humanitarian spirit. But is traditional "zoo life" our best course of action for these dispossessed creatures of the wild who have done nothing at all to deserve their fate? I propose, urgently so, an alternative — an abrupt detour to another place. And so I say to the reader, to zoo administrators, zoologists, biologists, and botanists in the front lines of caring for these animals, and especially to all wild animals who are driven from their native haunts or who are now captive and suffering the injustices of unnatural confinement — *please enter Zoo Paradise . . .*

[1]International Union for Conservation of Nature (September 2016 report).

CHAPTER ONE
A Question of Vitality

I remember the year, 1952, when my father took me to the San Diego Zoo, part of the Balboa Park complex in the center of town, and not far from my earliest boyhood home along the still undeveloped Mission Bay. The interesting hilly pathways that wove through the park, the forest like setting, the strange plants in the contrived man-made understory, the sights and sounds and smells of exotic animals (including the stench of copious amounts of dung) I had never seen nor heard of until then, contributed to the excitement and imagination of a young five year old boy. I could hardly wait to see it all — and I think I recall my father saying more than once, "Stay close, and don't be running off!" But maybe because I have always been a sensitive sort, it wasn't long before I began to sense a morbid darkness about the place that I have held within me ever since. That moment arrived unexpectedly when we finally reached the enormous ape enclosure.

Outside their cage, were two sculptures that my father took notice of and read to me. They commemorated two gorillas — captured in 1931 as youngsters in the Belgian Congo (today, the Democratic Republic of the Congo) and sold to the zoo by wildlife adventurers Martin and Osa Johnson. I don't know why the Johnson's names have stuck with me all these years — like the numbers on my Army "dog tags" which I've also never forgotten. Perhaps because there are certain experiences and people that I would just as soon forget, forever, but can't. Those gorillas, "M'bongo" and "Ngagi," were paid for by San Diego brother and sister benefactors Robert and Ellen Browning Scripps.[1] M'Bongo died first, purportedly from "Valley Hay Fever" due to fungal spores in his hay bedding; four years later Ngagi passed at age 18 years. Researchers today believe that obesity, possibly diabetes,[2] likely played a complicating role in both of their early deaths. Gorillas commonly live to 40 years and some beyond 50 in the wild. But they were the first of the "giant apes" brought to the zoo, and were so honored along with the Johnsons and the Scripps on those sculptures. Other gorillas soon took their place in 1949 under the lobbying influence of the zoo's naturalist, Belle Benchley. Actually, it is not my purpose to focus only upon these two gorillas, so allow me to briefly conclude my point, and then work forward from there to other animals held

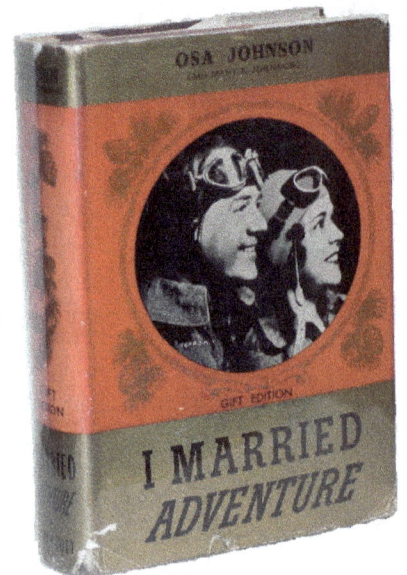

1940 best seller by Osa Johnson.

[1] One or both as benefactors of the earliest incarnations of the Scripps Institute (1924) and Scripps Institution of Oceanography (1902).

[2] More likely what I have identified as "Whole Body Inflammatory Disease" in my book, *Laminitis: A Plague of Unconscionable Proportions* (2017, NHC Press).

4

The San Diego Zoo in Balboa Park, San Diego, California, houses over 3,700 animals of more than 650 species and subspecies. San Diego Zoo pioneered the concept of open-air, cageless exhibits that re-create natural animal habitats. Or so they say!

captive in today's zoos, and, thence, to the purpose of this book.

Immediately behind the gorilla memorials was a glass partition, which separated the public from the many great apes that lived in divided enclosures behind the glass. So my father explained, the purpose of the partition was to prevent apes from flinging their feces at gawking visitors! Why would apes do such a thing? Well, if we look beyond them to the many other animals also living in close confinement at the zoo — relative to their true adaptive habitats in which their species evolved — boredom, isolation and separation from their natural world would be enough to make any wild animal (and how about humans?) go "stir crazy." And, as I've since learned, and witnessed myself, engage in chronic masturbation, lie motionless on the ground in depression, and become dissociative and dangerous to others apes, zoo keepers, and themselves. Newspapers are replete with such stories year after year. Google it, in case you're dubious.

But an important premise of creating zoos, like the one in Balboa Park, was, and is to this day (I returned to visit the zoo two years ago), to conduct scientific research, provide important sanctuaries for species facing eminent extinction in the wild, *and* educate people about living things that come from far off distant lands. And, in so doing, inculcate an appreciation of nature that they might otherwise never see nor experience. Nonetheless, when you come right down to it, modern zoos are still claustrophobic "jails" at worst, and, at best, boring cul-de-sacs of inactivity where the animal inmates are afforded "turn out" in limited spaces — even acreage! — but with little incentive to do anything

Giraffes at the West Midland Safari Park, Worcestershire, England.

but mope, wait for the next meal, and tune out non-stop hordes of noisy gawkers, zoo workers manning heavy equipment, tour buses, and tourist curio shops. Not a whole lot different in the mind of a wild animal than their species faced in 18th century menageries sealed in cement-walled pits, iron cages, and not oft chained to a wall or stake in the ground. While open acreage zoos of today may look good to humans — such as the north San Diego County Wild Animal Park that is also run by the same administrators of the Balboa Park zoo — they are, while more humane on some level, still amusement parks that cater more to the recreational pursuits of curious humans, than the actual biological needs and vitality of the animal inmates.

6,000 years of royal menageries, zoological gardens and safari parks

The first known zoos date back to 3500 BCE in Ancient Egypt, and amounted to animal collections called *menageries* owned by royalty. Royal menageries were the predecessors of the modern zoo — or, technically speaking, "zoological garden" — and some animals could be deployed in brutal public spectacles of trans-species combat. The 19th-century historian W.E.H. Lecky wrote of the Roman games, first held in 366 BCE:

> At one time, a bear and a bull, chained together, rolled in fierce combat across the sand . . . Four hundred bears were killed in a single day under Caligula . . . Under Nero, four hundred tigers fought with bulls and elephants. In a single day, at the dedication of the Colosseum by Titus, five thousand

Excavation of the Colosseum, 70/72 - 80 DC in Rome. Exposed is an elaborate underground structure called the *hypogeum*, which consisted of a two-level subterranean network of tunnels and cages beneath the arena where gladiators and animals were held before contests began. Exotic wild beasts from the far reaches of the Roman Empire were brought to Rome and hunts were held in the morning prior to the afternoon main event of gladiatorial duels. During the inauguration of the Colosseum over 9,000 animals were killed.

> animals perished. Under Trajan . . . lions, tigers, elephants, rhinoceroses, hippopotami [sic], giraffes, bulls, stags, even crocodiles and serpents were employed to give novelty to the spectacle.[1]

Menageries slowly evolved into public zoos, the earliest arriving during the Age of Enlightenment ("Age of Reason", commencing from the late 17th-century). These were marginally "educational events" serving to entertain and provide inspiration, using royal menageries. Others were also used for scientific and medical research.[2] Eventually public zoos formed in their own right, such as the *Tiergarten Schönbrunn or* "Vienna Zoo," the oldest zoo in the world still in operation today. Created in 1752 initially as a menagerie, it became public domain only after the dissolution of the Austro-Hungarian Empire following WWI. As late as the mid-20th Century, some public zoos even included human exhibits! Ota Benga, a Congolese pygmy, a "freed" 19th century slave, was displayed in 1906 in cages wrestling with different apes, portrayed as an "example of the 'missing link' between the orangutan and white man."[3] Most zoos during this early period amounted to animals living alone in cells or cages with bars, or in cement-walled pits in

[1]Lecky, W.E.H. *History of European Morals from Augustus to Charlemagne. Vol. I*, Longmans, 1869, pp. 280-282.
[2]Costello, John (June 9, 2011). *The great zoo's who*. Irish Independent.
[3]Bradford, Phillips Verner and Blume, Harvey. *Ota Benga: The Pygmy in the Zoo*. St. Martins Press, 1992.

(*Top left clockwise*) This chimpanzee was passed around five zoos before arriving in a Texas roadside zoo at the age of 37. Ota Benga, a former slave and here a human exhibit in New York, 1906. Juvenile elephant chained and sleeping in his paddock at zoo. Such notorious — but still acceptable — forms of confinement are conducive to anxiety, depression, and pathology.

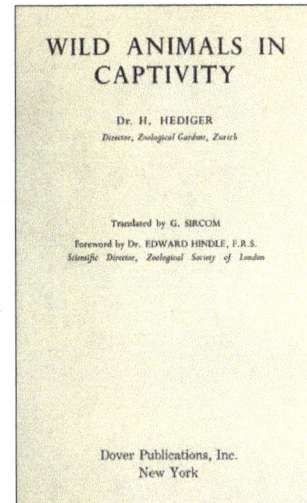

(Top, left) Carl Hagenbeck (June 10, 1844 - April 14, 1913) was a German merchant of wild animals who supplied many European zoos, as well as P.T. Barnum. He created the modern zoo with animal enclosures without bars that were closer to their natural habitat. *(Center)* Heini Hediger (1908-1992) was a Swiss biologist noted for work in *proxemics* (nonverbal communication) in animal behavior and is known as the "father of zoo biology". *(Right)* Still in print and available for purchase at online book outlets, Hediger's 1950 observations of wild animals in zoological gardens.

the ground, or chained to fixed objects. There was little or nothing natural at all about their miserable lives in captivity. And worse yet, some animals, deemed genetically inappropriate, "surplus," or "too old," might be euthanized, passed from zoo to zoo, auctioned off to hunting ranches, or simply dumped and abandoned at the side of a rural road like a piece of trash.

Concerns regarding unnatural confinement systems adversely affecting captive wild animals did not escape the pioneers of modern zoos. The German "animal collector" Carl Hagenbeck was one of the earliest, perhaps the first, of zookeepers who decried blatantly inhumane living conditions for captive animals and then did something about it. In 1907, Hagenbeck, envisioning animal enclosures that were more natural, opened the "Tierpark Hagenbeck," which revolutionized future zoo designs: instead of bars and cages, he built moats around paddocks to separate animals from each other and the public. In 1942 the Swiss biologist and ethologist Heini Hediger developed the science of zoo biology, which held that the life of animals in their natural surroundings must be studied in order to provide them with more natural living conditions during captivity. Today, Hagenbeck-style zoos like the San Diego Zoo at Balboa Park still predominate around the world, but a new generation of "Safari Parks" are on the rise, such as the aforementioned San Diego north county Wild Animal Park and the new 2,000 acre North Carolina Zoo which houses over 1,100 animals representing 200 species, and includes over 5 miles of walking paths (for people), air trams, and air-conditioned buses.[1] But even these "giants" are not without problems.

Belle Benchley's 1952 successor at the San Diego Zoo, Dr. Charles Schroeder, a veterinarian and pathologist, recognized the limits of the Balboa park's facility. Amid much lobbying of city fathers and voters for funding, Schroeder laid the vision and foundation for the north county San Diego Wild Animal Park (aka, San Diego Zoo Safari Park). In keeping with the visions and science of Hagenbeck and Hediger, he had engineered innovations at the city Balboa zoo, replacing cages with moats, creating a flamingo lagoon, and a great climbing stairway for apes (which did not exist as I recall at the time of my childhood visit), among other things. But in 1959 came his vision for the north county park, eventually created in 1970, a few months before Schroeder retired, described by one author as a "broad panorama of arbors, grasslands, watering holes, ponds, corrals, hills, and cliffs." But the otherwise adroit Schroeder would, nevertheless, see even its shortcomings, later lamenting:

> Our gorilla exhibit at the Wild Animal Park is one of the largest anywhere. But
> it's not enough. Animals need space to move and to run, to explore new areas,
> to climb and do all the things that come naturally. There isn't enough room for
> that. When you speak of the zoo in Balboa Park, there is nowhere for them to
> go. There are ninety-two acres locked in. It's bigger than zoos used to be. Let's
> face it; there were times when you had a tiger in an area sixteen feet by eight feet
> deep. Anybody knows that's not adequate for a tiger, and there's lots of zoos that have beauti-
> ful tiger exhibits, and they're pretty big, but they are inadequate. No, the Park is not even
> enough, but we've tried. The idea of putting animals in their natural settings is not new, but the

presentation is. The free-ranging animals move in herds, not in pairs, as in most zoos.[1]

What Schroeder recognized is that no matter how big the zoo or animal park might happen to be, once you put a fence around it and separate the animals, they know they are "caged" and will not move or behave naturally. To Schroeder, something was clearly missing in the "make it natural" Hagenbeck-Hediger axis. The obvious answer, of which he was fully aware, is "vitality." The question is, how do we as humanitarian care advocates and providers inspire and deliver it?

[1]Douglas G. Myers with Lynda Rutledge Stephenson, *Master Zoo—The Life and Legacy of Dt. Charles Schroeder* (Zoological Society of San Diego. 1999). 175-176.

CHAPTER TWO

Trekking In Wild Horse Country

The insidious health issues associated with close-confinement of zoo animals have not escaped me in my own professional work with horses. During the 1970s, I served horse owners as a farrier (horseshoer), but since the 1980s, I came to serve horses as a "natural hoof care (NHC) practitioner." So the reader understands, farriers nail (or sometimes glue) horseshoes to the horse's foot. NHC practitioners don't citing widespread evidence that shoeing harms the horse's foot, and that horses prosper going barefoot as nature intended. Nevertheless, in both capacities, it was my practice to travel from one boarding facility to another to take care of horses' feet. But this peripatetic practice also enabled me to see what happens to horses in the broadest sense when they are locked up in stalls or small paddocks — or even turned out onto grass pastures, which most people today believe is perfectly natural for horses (surprisingly, they are not!). Not only did I learn that shoeing itself caused great harm to the horse's foot, but that "stall life" (and pasture life, equally so) took an even greater toll on the entire animal. It was evident to me and others in my profession also working in the trenches that disease and lameness was — and still is — widespread among horses living in domestication. My concerns were later echoed by another farrier Walt Taylor, co-founder of the American Farriers Association, and a member of the World Farriers Association and Working Together for Equines programs, and is worth sharing here:

> Of the 122 million equines found around the world, no more than 10 percent are clinically sound. Some 10 percent (12.2 million) are clinically, completely and unusably lame. The remaining 80 percent (97.6 million) of these equines are somewhat lame . . . and could not pass a soundness evaluation or test.[1]

Sensitive to the suffering of animals under any circumstance, I began to question not only what I was doing as a "hoof man," but the very foundations of modern horse management. Surely, I reasoned, nature did not error in creating the horse with doomed hooves and bodily breakdown after 55 million years of evolutionary descent!

In 1982, chance would have it that one of my clients in the San Francisco Bay Area adopted a wild horse (mare) from our government's Wild Horse & Burro Program — administrated by the Bureau of Land Management (BLM), the U.S. Forest Service, and the National Park Service. Only a week before she had been plucked out of the back country of Nevada during one of the BLM's notorious, albeit legal, "gathers." Asked by

---

[1][American Farriers Journal, Nov./2000, v. 26, #6, p. 5.]

Wild horses are ushered into a holding pen during a gather. Typically, the BLM releases a trained horse, dubbed a "Judas horse", ahead of the fleeing horses who are pushed along towards their destination by a helicopter. Today, as many horses are held in long term holding corrals as there are remaining on public rangelands.

my client to take a look at her feet to see if they needed trimming, I was totally flabbergasted by what I saw: hooves so perfectly formed and durable, I could only imagine (given my then farrier perspective) that the animal who wore them was a mutant freak, or of an alien species from another planet! Less than a week later, I found my way into the U.S. Great Basin, home to America's wild, free-roaming horses, for I had to know how this was possible.

The clash between my work at the hoof and what I knew about horses living in domestication, and what I found in the Herd Management Areas (HMAs) of the BLM spun me completely out of control as a professional.[1] My life would be changed forever. Nature's "model" for "natural care" lie before me. And, to this end, over the next four years I ambitiously studied their hooves, their natural habitat, and the lifestyle that rendered these animals so healthy, in short, what constituted their "vitality." I came to know the species in an entirely new reality: an animal full of health and motivation, one living in stark contrast to the pathetic parody inhabiting the barns and pastures I knew I could no longer serve "business as usual." Increasingly, I became haunted by the awareness that I was contributing to the suffering of another living being. Without knowing it, I had

---

[1] The BLM estimates that 40,605 wild horses and burros roamed in 179 Herd Management Areas in 10 states: Arizona, California, Colorado, Idaho, Montana, Nevada, New Mexico, Oregon, Utah, and Wyoming.

In their natural world, the horse thinks and behaves as nature intended. 55 million years of natural selection defines what this is. I believe the NHC model brings us closer to the truth. I can understand, however, why advocates of conventional horsemanship believe otherwise. When the horse's head, mouth, and throat are trussed and choked with steel, pulleys, nooses and levers acting like a straight-jacket, his feet clamped and nailed tight with steel shoes, and then whipped, drugged, fed like a human diabetic, and prevented from moving freely, naturally and *without pain*, one can believe just about anything they want.

essentially aligned myself intuitively with the "Hagenbeck Revolution" and the still nascent zoological science of Hediger. Today, there is a saying in our "NHC Revolution": once we've arrived via the epiphany of the wild horse model, "there's no turning back."

In 1992, *The Natural Horse: Lessons from the Wild,* my first book on the subject of equine natural care — based on equine life in the wild as I had come to know it — was published by Northland Publishing (Flagstaff, Arizona). Since then, I have authored eleven more related books, contributed many technical and lay articles for the American Farriers Journal and equestrian magazines, lectured at scientific symposiums in the U.S. and abroad, and hosted more educational and training clinics than I can remember. My findings in wild horse country revealed incredibly invaluable lessons for humane domestic horse care, which left me no choice but to publish, lecture, teach, and advocate about

Living alone in the "slaves quarters".

it — a life's work that continues to this day.

The horse, *Equus ferus caballus*, evolved into his modern form 1.4 million years ago.[1,2] A prey species, they live naturally in close knit family bands that need freedom to move 24/7 if they are to be healthy ("vitality"). Lock them up, isolate them from each other, and a myriad of debilitating physical and turbulent psychological problems erupt. Add the pernicious effects of an unnatural diet, unnatural feeding practices, unnatural hoof care, and unnatural horsemanship, and the outcome cannot be better expressed than in Taylor's afore cited indictment of the horse-using community. Not surprisingly, few people are aware of this "equine holocaust," as it has become culturally acceptable, a mindset, if you will. Virtually every book and article on the subject of horsemanship, every equestrian association, and every movie rolled out by Hollywood has portrayed the horse variously as a child's plaything, racing machine, gallant slave, and even "dangerous

[1] Worth reading are Kirkpatrick and Fazio in *Wild Horses as Native North American Wildlife*. The authors write, "According to the work of researchers from Uppsala University of the Department of Evolutionary Biology (Forstén 1992), the date of origin, based on mutation rates for mitochondrial-DNA, for *E. caballus*, is set at approximately 1.7 million years ago in North America. This, of course, is very close, geologically speaking, to the 1-2 million-year figure presented by the interpretation of the fossil record." Kirkpatrick, J.F., and P.M. Fazio. Revised January 2010. *Wild Horses as Native North American Wildlife*. The Science and Conservation Center, ZooMontana, Billings. P. 3.

[2] More on the specie's ancient lineage: Weinstock, J.; *et al.* (2005). "Evolution, Systematics, and Phylogeography of Pleistocene horses in the New World: A Molecular Perspective". *PLoS Biology* 3 (8): e241. Orlando, L.; *et al.* (2008). "Ancient DNA Clarifies the Evolutionary History of American Late Pleistocene Equids". *Journal of Molecular Evolution* 66 (5): 533–538. Cai, Dawei; Zhuowei Tang, Lu Han, Camilla F. Speller, Dongya Y. Yang, Xiaolin Ma, Jian'en Cao, Hong Zhu, Hui Zhou (2009). "Ancient DNA Provides New Insights into the Origin of the Chinese Domestic Horse". *Journal of Archaeological Science* 36 (3): 835–842. Vilà, Carles; Jennifer A. Leonard, Anders Götherström, Stefan Marklund, Kaj Sandberg, Kerstin Lidén, Robert K. Wayne, Hans Ellegren (2001). [10.1126/science. 291.5503.474 "Widespread Origins of Domestic Horse Lineages"]. *Science* 291 (5503): 474–477.

predator." In any case, it is an animal coping with the demands of anthromorphistic humans, and typically living alone in "slave quarters" called "stalls." The notion that the horse might have some say in their own behalf in this slavish, utilitarian relationship with humans has been as wholly lost to the slaver as the recognition that the horse never asked for any of it in the first place. In fact, it has become "politically correct" to say, "A horse needs a job." What a horse "needs" is a humane lifestyle with other horses.

Fortunately, 37 years since I entered wild horse country, an entire movement based on NHC has arisen in the world of the domestic horse to make his life more natural, and, therefore, more humane. It hasn't been easy, and the struggle to educate others about the foundational value of NHC continues to this very moment. But there is no turning back to my former ways, and I am forever grateful to, and humbled by, our wild horses, who have shed badly needed light on the true meaning of humane care. And all along this journey, I have never forgotten the parallel plight of animals incarcerated in zoos (some much worse than others!). I have even gone public on this at speaking engagements, because I really see no difference in the inhumanity of unnatural habitats wherever they are: horse stables, zoos, breeding farms, backyards, and even pet stores. So my advocacy has extended to all animals who are deprived of their liberty, native lifestyles and natural habitats. Healthful alternatives are not only needed, humans are more than capable of rising to the occasion and doing something about it.

But, if I am an advocate, I am equally a pragmatist. I am not one to complain about anything if I am unwilling to make an effort to confront the problem and work towards a solution. And so it was from my experiences in studying equine life in the wild, that came the vision for what I call "natural boarding" popularized today in my fifth book, *Paddock Paradise: A Guide to Natural Horse Boarding* (2005). The concept is remarkably simple, but its complexity lies in the applications of what I call the "lessons from the wild." These are the behavioral *stimuli* that give vitality to wild horses in the HMAs, and that we can simulate in Paddock Paradise. In the wild, horses move along well worn paths that lead from one place and activity to another. What happens along these paths are the "lessons from the wild." Horse owners are challenged in *Paddock Paradise* to simulate these by creating a *track* around their property, within which horses create their own *paths*, and by providing behavioral-based stimuli along the way to help encourage the horses to live naturally like their brethren in the wild. Today, Paddock Paradises are now dotting the international equestrian landscape, turning lives of misery into lifestyles of unprecedented vitality.[1]

---

[1]No one knows for sure how many Paddock Paradises there are to date, but the numbers of horses inhabiting them is surely in the thousands and growing based on horse owners reporting into Paddock Paradise Facebook page. The concept has caught on internationally, and the book has been translated into nearly a dozen languages. Be sure to visit: www.PaddockParadise.net to learn more.

Extraordinary photograph of numerous adult wolves, drawn from different family packs, converging and traveling single file on one path as they make their way to a buffalo hunt in wintry Yellowstone National Park.

In the wild, I learned that horses are not the only species using paths (*Overleaf*). Deer, antelope, free-roaming cattle, bears, wolves, elephants, and many other species, use them. In effect, they are "highways" for efficient travel as very busy animals move here and there to meet their survival needs. We can engineer these tracks in zoos, as in Paddock Paradise, and pepper them with appropriate triggers to get the animals moving as naturally as horses do in Paddock Paradise and in wild horse country.

The inherent value of the Paddock Paradise concept to zoos lies in its trans-species adaptability and the promise of vitality. The great challenge will be to transpose and integrate the "lessons from the wild" derived from each species into Zoo Paradise. This, I imagine, will require the cooperative import of knowledge and skills of visionaries, artists, zoologists, biologists, botanists, engineers, carpenters, environmentalists, and others — actually, the very same people who have created and then run public zoos. To some extent, horse owners and NHC practitioners like myself have pioneered that path for equines (including zebras!). Untold numbers of horses worldwide are now reaping the genuine benefits of "natural boarding" in a myriad of Paddock Paradise themes. Paddock Paradise is, and always will be, a "work in progress" and, I predict, so will Zoo Paradise. Nature is vast in its possibilities and in the opportunities it affords us, if only we will try.

The fundamental question every advocate should raise above all and foremost in any

Overleaf: Tracks and paths.

(Continued on page 20)

What is a "track?" What is a "path?"

I think of *paths* as "wildlife highways" often shared by multiple species, whether solo or in family bands, leading from one activity (e.g., a feeding or hunting ground) to another (e.g., watering hole). It was clear to me in my vision for Paddock Paradise that paths would have their place too. One question I faced early on was who should forge them — me or the horses? At best, a compromise was inevitable because I realized that the paths would have to navigate through the myriad possibilities and limitations of different properties horse owners had to work with. This meant necessarily that people would have to direct the general locations of the paths, but surely the horses themselves could pinpoint their exact locations according to their instincts? From this quandary distilled the concept of the *track* — a swath across the property created by the horse owner *within* which the horses would determine the exact location and dimensions of their paths. I put it to the test at the AANHCP Field Headquarters, and not only did it happen as envisioned, I came to really appreciate how significant "pathing" is in the psyche of horses — even in captivity. I'll weigh in on this further in the Chapter 3 tour of our AANHCP Paddock Paradise where I provide examples of just how important it is to them. It almost goes without saying that Zoo Paradise administrators will also face the same issue. Happily, it is readily soluble through "tracking" and "pathing" — humans and animals working together in harmony with each others respective technical and biological requirements.

(*Facing page*) Elephant "on path" in central Africa. Poaching, encroaching civilization, and civil war are increasingly taking an enormous toll on these (and other) wild animals and their natural habitat. Zoologists can help prepare the way for their survival when politicians, environmentalists, and wildlife advocates fail to turn the tide, by laying the groundwork for Zoo Paradise *now*. It is of paramount importance to sustain their vitality following the inevitable and traumatizing transition from the wild into captivity, and giving them a robust life "on track, on paths" in Zoo Paradise.

(Continued from page 17)

such endeavor is this: *what is a healthy animal?* Indeed, what is the meaning of "vitality"? As I learned back in 1982 and have advocated ever since — really echoing the admonitions of Hediger — the answer lies in each specie's adaptive environment and indigenous lifestyle. But today, the natural world is under siege by human encroachment and plunder. In fact, many zoos have taken stock of this and are working with governments and wildlife advocates, opening their facilities as safe havens for species threatened with annihilation and extinction. Since this ominous trend seems inevitable, we should do what we can to help the animals' denouement in captivity as close to what is natural for them as possible. And what better way than to draw upon the expertise of our scientists, advocates, and supportive humanitarians to deliver — with a sense of urgency — the promise of vitality in the concept Zoo Paradise?

Before identifying and portraying those "lessons from the wild" that will turn "misery into vitality" in this book's vision for Zoo Paradise, I want to lay the foundations for the Paddock Paradise concept that became a reality for our horses at the AANHCP Field Headquarters along the central coast of California (USA).* Then in the next chapter, we will take a tour of that Paddock Paradise with the lessons applied, paving the way for Zoo Paradise.

*Guided tours of the AANHCP Paddock Paradise were conducted for nearly seven years, before our lease ended in 2017.

Creating a Paddock Paradise

While most any size property beyond one acre in size will work, let's say, for discussion, that you own 5 acres and 6 horses. For effect, let's also say that the five acres has a sturdy perimeter fence, and is planted in a combination of woods and lush green grasses, the latter known to cause laminitis — one of the deadliest and debilitating diseases of horses known today. In other words, by filling in the previous diagram a bit, we now have something like this:

Paddock Paradise has a sturdy perimeter fence to contain the horses. It may be forested and planted in lush green grasses, as is the case here with this 5 acre tract— a deadly founder trap until Paddock Paradise changes everything.

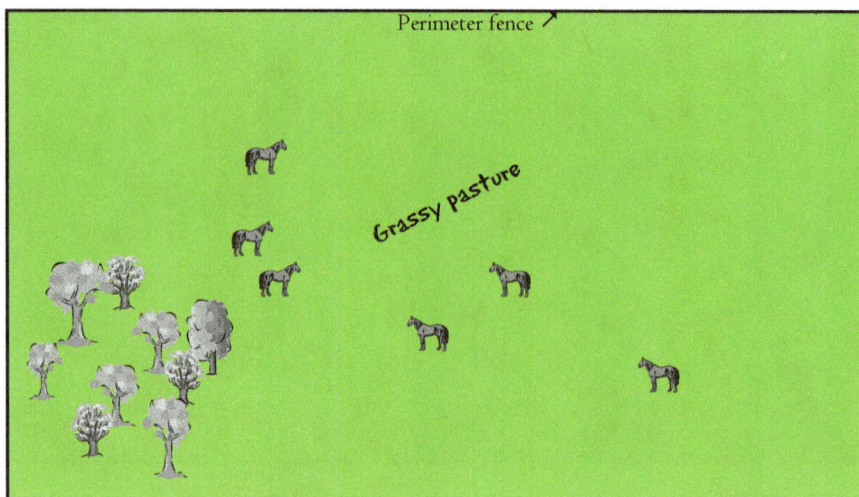

Perimeter fence

Grassy pasture

Obviously, we can't leave our horses stranded in there with this kind of threat! Ah, but we can, and this is where Paddock Paradise comes in. The first thing we want to do is create a second fence line *inside* the perimeter fence. This will be an electric fence, and we will place it approximately 10 to 15 feet away from the perimeter fence. Now, the horses are contained within two fences: a sturdy, stationary perimeter fence and an inner adjustable electric fence:

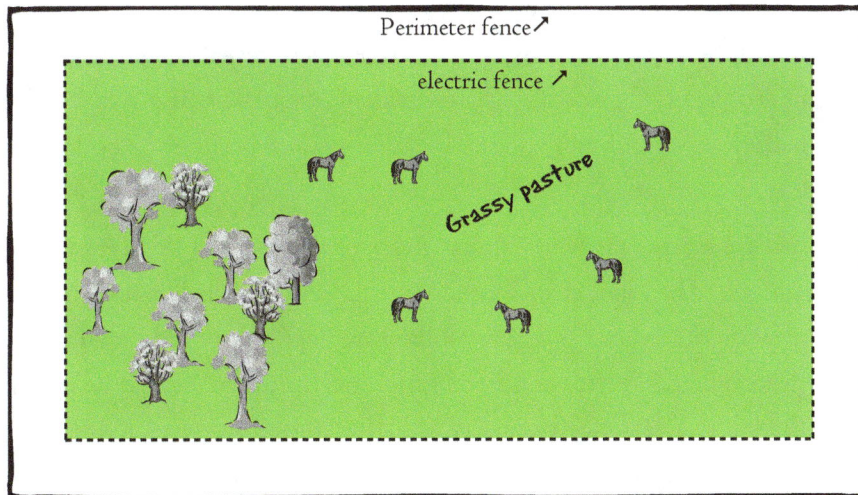

Creating the "track."

It doesn't take long for the horses to learn to stay clear of the electric fence either. The electric fence will soon play an important role in Paddock Paradise. Okay, we are now ready to place the horses inside Paddock Paradise, and "on track". And it's as simple as this:

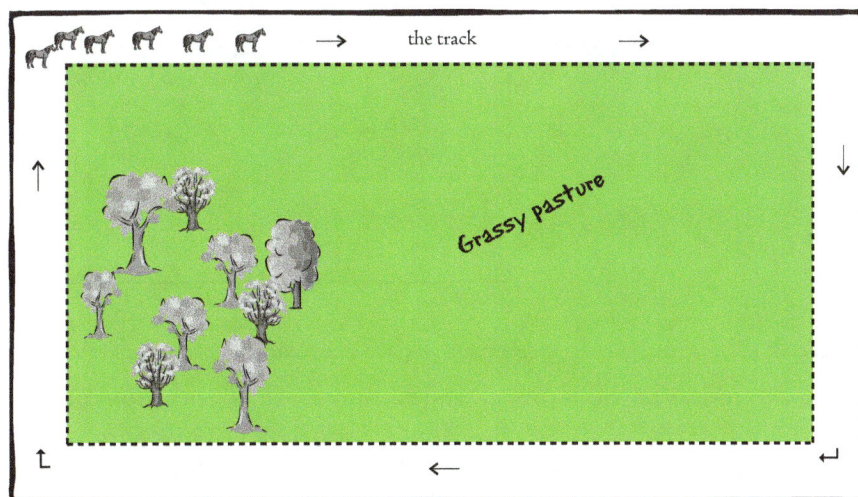

Horses "on track."

Although we've not even begun to flesh out the many possible features of Paddock Paradise at this stage, we now know from experience that horses begin to move out immediately on track! The impetus to move is instigated by the animal's innate curiosity towards anything that is new, particularly anything to do with their living quarters. "What is this and where does it lead to?" is probably running through the equine mind. And the solution is obvious to them too — simple movement to go check it out. We capitalize on this group curiosity (no one wants to be left behind either in wild horse country or in Paddock Paradise!) by building in specific *stimuli* that will tend to keep the horses looking forward to moving along naturally as a family type band, or as a herd of family bands.

Now that we have our horses on track, a situation may arise where a member of the family band gets separated from the others who by one means or another left the track leaving the horse alone. What happens next is actually very revealing of the equine mind and how their perception of space is so different than ours. We will use that difference in planning the behavioral stimuli in Paddock Paradise — and no doubt Zoo Paradise as well.

Among the five escapees is your "alpha" mare,[1] who temporarily keeps the "herd" close to the paddock. The loner is anxious about this, and nervously paces the fence line wishing he were with the others. Now the alpha mare decides to head down the lane to visit your neighbor's herd. The loner becomes hysterical, and we see that he may even decide to jump the fence — a dangerous move as he might become ensnared in the barbed wire or whatever the fence is comprised of. Now we cut open the fence line for him to make his escape, and announce the fact to him:

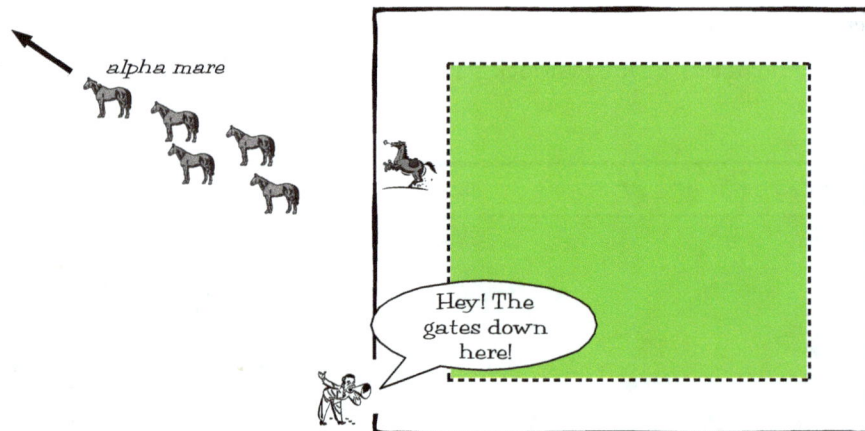

But, we notice that he cannot even perceive the gate no matter how much we yell the fact to him or point to it. His cognitive mind cannot compute the information or the reality.

---

[1]"Horse families travel in distinct hierarchal formations, ordered according to relative dominance ('pecking order'). Typically, there is a dominant 'alpha' (also called 'monarch') stallion positioned at the rear of the band, urging forward movement as necessary, where he is able to keep a defensive eye on his family, and fending off competitive males in the area as challenges arise. Then there is his favorite mare — generally the 'alpha' female — leading most band movements from the front. Also, commonly, there are one or more other harem mares subdominant ('beta') to the alpha mare. And, too, the young offspring, always at or near the mother's side. Finally, and kept by the alpha stallion at an acceptable distance away from his herd, a pack of 'bachelor' stallions (also ordered according to relative dominance) not yet aggressive enough to claim their own females. Possibly also nearby are one or more 'allied' harem bands, led by their alpha stallions but who are subdominant to the monarch described above." [*Paddock Paradise*, p. 19.]

Not until he paces down the fence line far enough to where he actually stumbles upon the opening will he recognize it — and make his escape to join the others. But once he does, he will never forget it! Put him or any horse in the same situation and whether a second, minute, day, month or year later, he will immediately run to that spot in the fence line, regardless if the gate is still there or not, to try and get out. It may be a fence with a gate to us, but in the equine mind, it is only an obstacle with an opening to get through. Humans and horses process information differently.

And on this point, too, hinges the entire premise of Zoo Paradise. Space must be configured with opportunities — "triggers" — that will precipitate natural behavioral responses from each animal that occur in the wild. These triggers are specifically the "lessons from the wild". I believe the problem with most accepted animal confinement systems today is that they either outright obstruct or preclude such responses, or reward the animal to disengage from them — issues I will discuss later in this text in the context of preventive care. Either way, the animal fails to behave naturally, and, as mentioned earlier, a plethora of problems, from the mind to the foot, then erupt: depression, neurotic behaviors (e.g., "stall vices" and self-mutilization), and inability to engage in natural socialization patterns (pecking order, family band, herd dynamics, and symbiotic trans-species interactions); metabolic disorders, including cancer, diabetes, and life-threatening diseases of the foot such as laminitis in equines (zebras, giraffes, elephants, and many other ungulates are equally vulnerable); and musculoskelature breakdown.[1] In my visits to zoos around the United States, these are issues I've observed, and they are not uncommon.

The way out of this conundrum is the "track," proven in Paddock Paradise for countless equines around the world. The track is the central "artery" of Paddock Paradise. It is the main thoroughfare along which we seek to propel the horse forward naturally, deploying "triggers" along the way to keep him going.

This then leads us to the promised "tour" of the AANHCP Paddock Paradise. From its inception in 2010 until closed down in 2017, our Paddock Paradise was a living experiment with exceptional vitality that inured to the horses 24/7. So, on this promising note, let us move to the next chapter and take a brief look at our healthy horses who lived together 24/7 — unattended by us 23 of those 24 hours — and always on track in "paradise" with virtually none of the problems that plague millions of horses suffering under the yoke of close confinement and "laminitis pasture traps" in the outer world of domesticity. From there, we will return to the zoological garden and see if we can't conjure a new and humane vision for its inhabitants' vitality based on the same premise of Paddock Paradise — the "lessons from the wild".

[1]For a discussion of laminitis from the NHC perspective, see my book *Laminitis: An Equine Plague of Unconscionable Proportions — Healing and protecting Your Horse Using Natural Care Principles & Practices* (2016).

CHAPTER THREE

Paddock Paradise: In Pursuit of Equine Vitality

Any vision or planning for a Paddock Paradise (like Zoo Paradise) starts with an evaluation of the land available and its inherent possibilities. This was the case at the AANHCP Field Headquarters, near Lompoc, California (USA) where 12 acres of ideal rocky coastal mountain land was converted into our official Paddock Paradise. Arid and dry most of the year, the land very much resembled the high desert biome of wild horse country in the U.S. Great Basin I had visited many times 35 years earlier. Of course, our choice of land was very much the opposite of what most horse owners, breeding operations, and boarding facilities would go for. Hollywood movies and television have pretty much conjured up the mythical landscape considered ideal for horses: stalls, small paddocks, and lush grass pastures flat as a pancake — typically based on fence lines meeting at "right angles". And that's what people by and large try to put together for their horses today. But none of this is natural for horses in any respect, and the clash with wild horse country — our model for humane boarding conditions — is striking. In this regard, Paddock Paradise — as will Zoo Paradise — represents an enormous paradigm shift in horse care. Foremost, the ideal Paddock Paradise property is ruggedly convoluted, arid, and with few things meeting at "right angles" anywhere. For this reason, Paddock Paradise land will be, relatively speaking, "cheap" land disdained by those who covet that fancy horse properties of convention. Happily, the shift, in life, is a relatively simple one to make if what is best for one's horse is the highest priority.

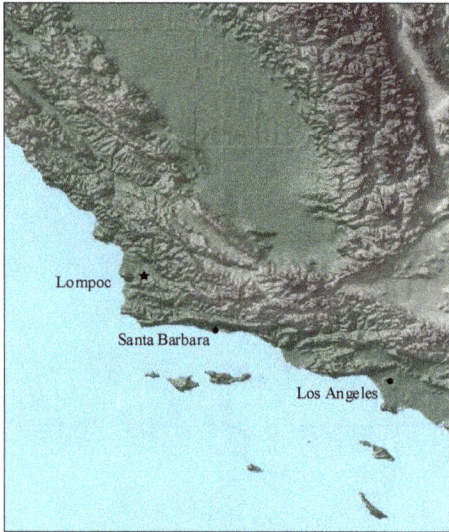

Before proceeding, I think it's important for readers to know that "stall life", seen here *(facing page)*, and small "turn out" paddocks, are typical of most "homes" for horses today around the world. Day in, day out, there is nothing to do and certainly with little or no physical contact with other horses. Stall life — tantamount to a person bound in a strait jacket living in a jail cell — is neither good nor natural for any horse. *Paddock Paradise*, as the following pages will reveal, is my answer to such unnatural bondage and boarding of horses.

But there are parallels that accord to today's zoos as well. In fact, systems of "close confinement" are systemic in most zoos today, including the large "wild animal parks," whose designs — we recall Schroeder lamenting — actually fail to stimulate vital psycho-

Tierpark Berlin (Zoo of Eastern Berlin), Germany.

logical and behavioral expression. Typically, in all cases we see isolated animals grubbing for extra forage, begging for handouts from gawking visitors, or laying about bored waiting for zoo feeding crews (*above*). As with stalled horses, this is no life for wild animals either, and Zoo Paradise is a ready made concept to right this wrong.

In the pages that follow in this chapter, we'll take a short tour of our Paddock Paradise at the AANHCP Field Headquarters. But this is only a snapshot of the enormous realm of possibilities inherent in the Paddock Paradise concept. Horse owners around the world today are doing marvelous things with it, and I remain in awe of my fellow human beings and the lengths they will go to on the behalf of the well-being of their treasured horses. And may zoo administrators follow suit with Zoo Paradise.

Far to the west of the U.S. Great Basin, along the central coast of California in the mountains just south of the small town of Lompoc, the AANHCP hosted a Paddock Paradise inspired by the system of paths used by wild horses of the Great Basin. In this aerial view of the property (*above*), a yellow line marks the location of a fenced "track" within which are paths created by our five resident horses. The entire track forms a one mile long loop, which rises 400 feet from the "water trough" at the lowermost point to "#3 Feed Station" (where we put out hay) at the very top. Let's meet the horses and then take a brief look at their lives in Paddock Paradise, beginning with several bird's-eye views of the track.

Meet our horses!

Five horses are the full-time residents of our Paddock Paradise, although there are occasional equine visitors who come for short stays for rehabilitation purposes. Apollo (*below*) is our senior "alpha" male at 29 years of age. Horses live in natural "pecking order" societies based on dominance. So, noting that, Apollo is at the top, next *(facing page)* comes Chakra (18 year old gelding), followed by Audrey (16 year old mare), then Chance (10 year old gelding), and finally Tess (10 year old mare). Chance and Tess are half brother-sister with the same father but different mothers. Audrey is Chance's mother. They are an extremely close-knit family, staying close together 24/7, just like family bands in the wild. Horses are animals of prey, so it is in their DNA to group together out of a sense of protection from predators. Mountain lions are natural predators of the horse, and one lives in close proximity of our track, so, as in the wild, our horses remain vigilant 24/7. Let's follow them "on track" to see what they are up to . . . but first, for the sake of orientation, let's look at a few photos representing the lay of the land.

Apollo

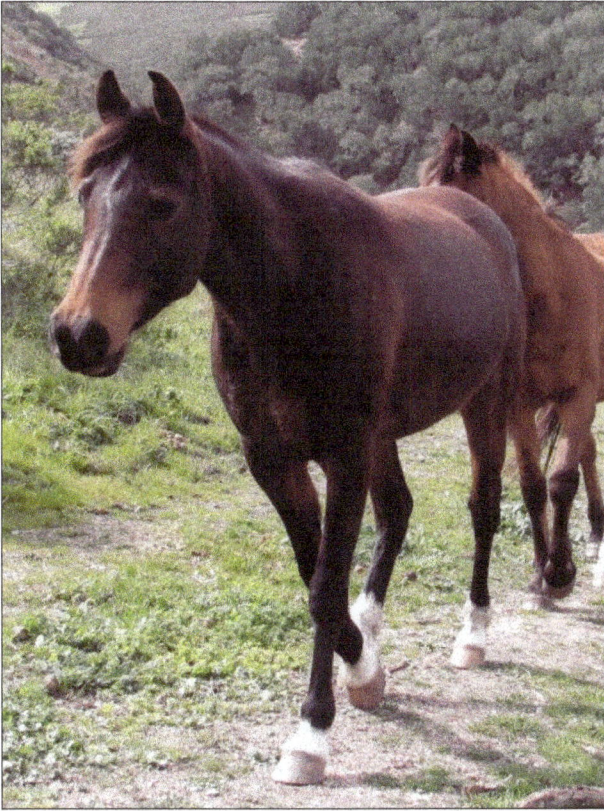

Audrey

Tess

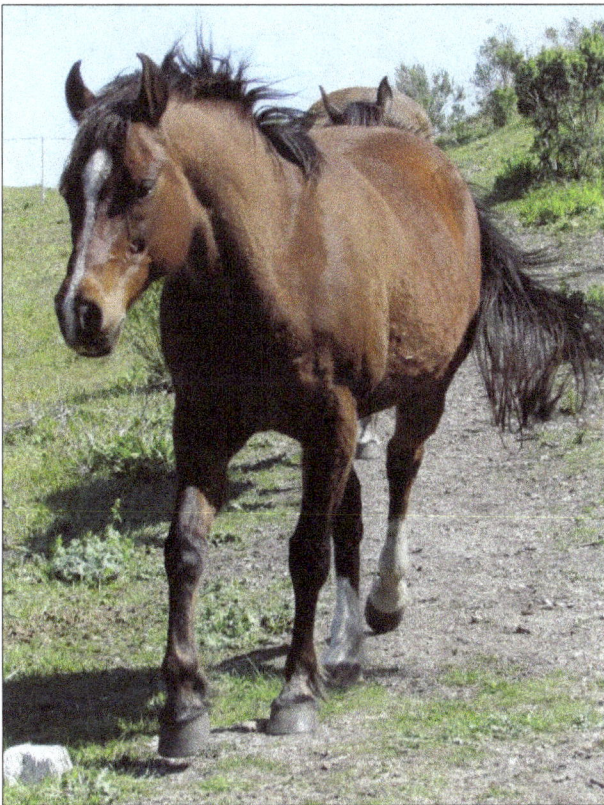

Chakra

Chance

View from the southeast. Horses group to forage at Feed Station #3; #4 is at lower right (*facing page*). *White arrow* [*inset map*] points in the direction this photo was taken.

View from the northwest. Feed Station #1 at lower center, #5 at upper right. Conventionally, horses would live inside the pasture not around its perimeter. But "pasture life" has its dangers, due to the presence of the sugar Fructan — a "trigger" for the life-threatening hoof disease known as "laminitis", a widespread equine plague.

White arrow [inset] is aimed in the direction of the view from Feed Station #3 down to #2 (lower left) and #5 (upper right). Seasonal grass has gone from moist and green to dry. But the horses continue their lives 24/7 on track, whatever the weather may bring.

White arrow [inset] points in the direction of this view. The horses are foraging at Feed Station #5. In principle and practice, Paddock Paradise is a tracking system with paths modeled after the movements of wild, free-roaming horses in their home ranges. Paddock Paradise facilitates both sexes and all ages living together, while encouraging species based natural movement and behaviors 24/7.

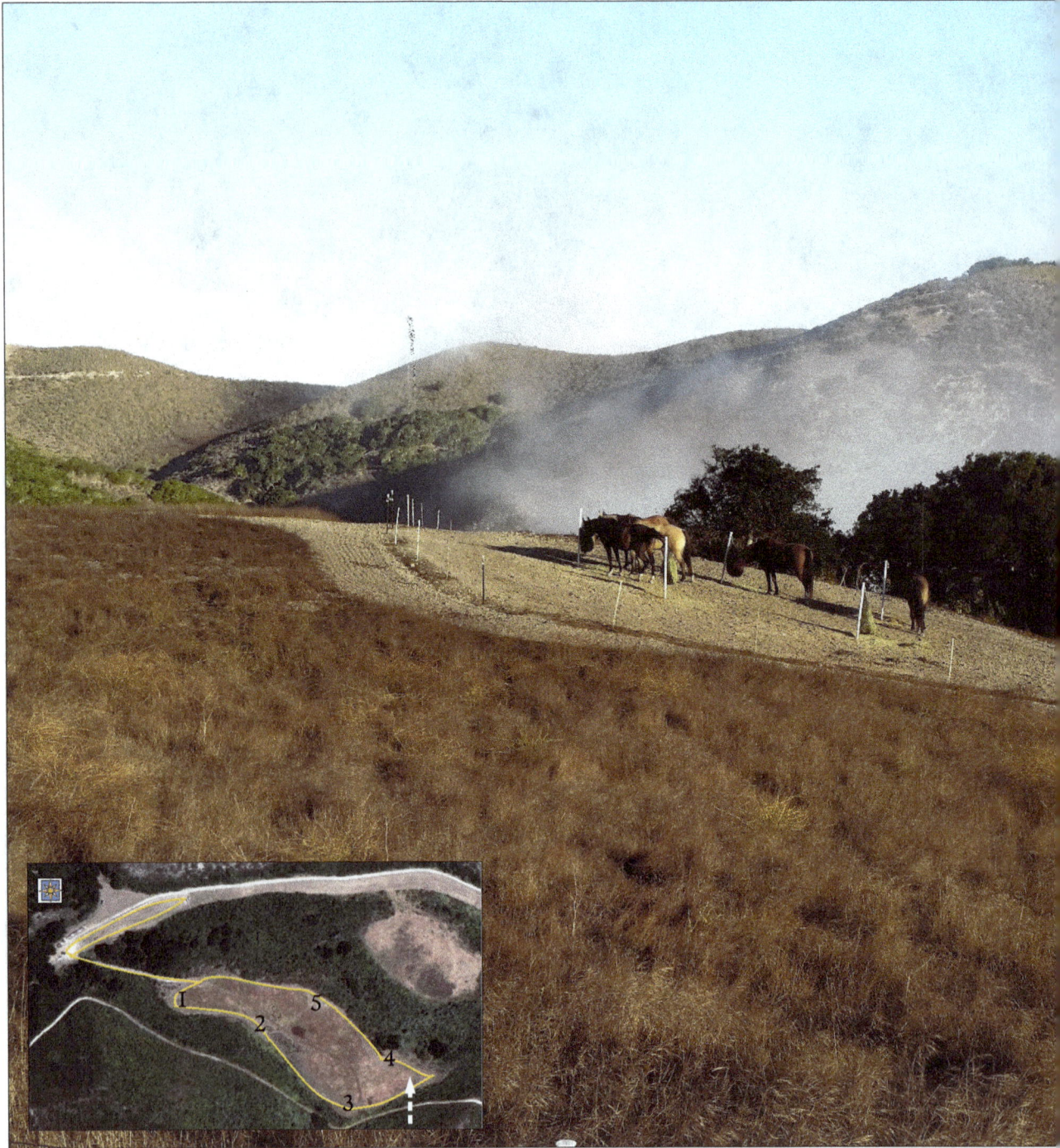

White arrow [inset] points direction of view.

Horses gather at Feed Station #4. Marine layer creeping in from nearby Pacific Ocean is almost a daily affair, along with powerful onshore winds. This, and much more, is to say that their family band structure, patterns of socialization, living out in the elements in a relatively rugged environment, eating a natural diet and in a natural way, and having the freedom to move when and where they please in their "home range", fits their species perfectly. In the wild, family bands I came to know were friendly, curious, sociable, and — once I understood their ground rules for mingling and getting to know them vis a vis — they were like being with any horse. In fact, it is the "naturalizing" of one's relationship with the horse that gives one a greater appreciation for their species. I believe this applies to all species when given the same relative opportunities to live their lives as nature intended. Zoo Paradise holds this promise.

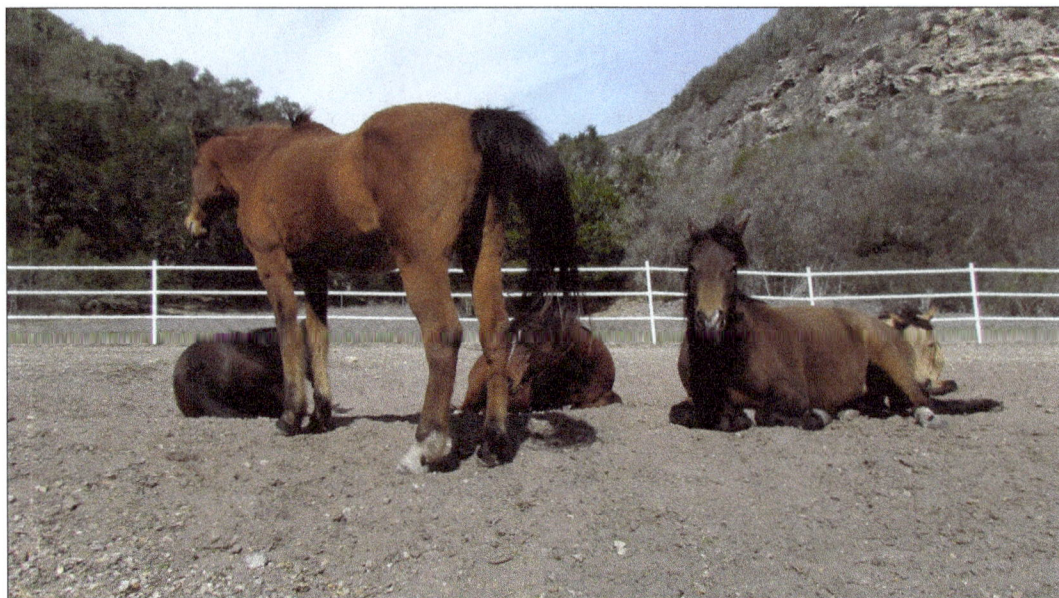

[*Note: star on map indicates location of tour discussions.*] Typically, on any given mid-morning, we find our family band napping and sleeping together at the sand pile in the lower field, so we'll commence our "official" tour here. This is also where much "rolling" behavior takes place. In the wild, family bands line-up in order of dominance to take their turn in these much favored spots.

Above, Apollo stands vigilant over his recumbent family, a job he reciprocates with Audrey, who will stand by while Apollo takes his turn. Contrary to popular myth, horses rest, but do not sleep, while standing — they must lie down to sleep. In the wild, mid-morning sleeping and napping are diurnal, and, accordingly, this is respected in Paddock Paradise. In contrast, the constant din of man-made noise pervades nearly every square inch of zoos midday. Only until nightfall arrives and visitors leave is there relative peace and quiet, save the chorus of animal cries for the evening meal. This feeding practice throws a troubling wrench into normal DNA–based nighttime prey-predator behavioral tensions, let alone sleepless days.

(*Facing page, above*) Chance, awakening, takes his turn rolling, as nearby family mates wait patiently — just like horses in the wild *(below)*!

Seasonal rains form water holes, both in the wild and here at the AANHCP Field Headquarters, where Chance and Tess are quenching their thirst.

In the wild (*above*) and at our Field Headquarters (*right*), horses will splash and soak themselves in water holes, then roll in dirt (or sand) caking their hides in mud. Other than the clear enjoyment of scratching one's back, the effect has biological significance as well: the mud forms a protective barrier against biting insects, healing "combat" wounds, and sustaining healthy, vibrant and glistening coats that most surely serve "sexual selection!"

Paths are everything to the horses in our Paddock Paradise. Paths cross link — through the animal's DNA — their ancient adaptive environment and their innate sense of survival to move repetitively over familiar ground: where they should go precisely and for what reason. Most horse owners today are completely oblivious to this powerful existential connection of land, survival and vitality in the mind of the horse. During the early days of the BLM's gathers in wild horse country, government wranglers on horse back found it nearly impossible to drive horses away from their rangeland paths to nearby "traps", antecedent to the current helicopter "round ups"— which, in effect, terrorize horses into captivity. As quick as the removal "pressure" to leave their paths was lifted, they would zoom right back to the familiar home range. I put this to the test at the AANHCP Field Headquarters: *(Above) Black arrow* points to path connecting the water trough and sand pit. *Blue arrow* on inset map shows the direction of the view. Seeing them use it daily, I "dragged" (see "drag" on page 59) it into oblivion one late afternoon, marking off and photographing its precise location beforehand. The next morning, to the inch, it was completely replicated!

(Above left) Wild horse family band moves "single file" in the Great Basin; hence, it comes as no surprise that we find the same type of depressed pathways as seen in the adjacent photo that has been frequented by many family/bachelor bands over many generations of wild horses.

(Below) Wildebeest family bands traverse in single file an African plain.

This is our open-sided "run in" shelter, which the horses may use for shade on the hottest days, or for temporary shelter from heavy rainfall. To enter it, it is up to them; as is their exit. I've been known to join them several times when heavy rains suddenly unload and I'm working in the lower field! To the average horse owner whose horse is living a stall life in a barn in the center of a city, the suggestion that their horse is in any way vulnerable to the species's apex predators, is incredulous. Yet, in the mind and biology of the horse, the possibility of a lurking predator is as real as the setting sun. Thus, if close-confined (e.g., in a stall), the horse lives with a steady under current of stress that is not natural for his species. My feeling is that this may exacerbate or be causal to chronic laminitis in many ungulates, horses and zoo animals alike, due to glucocorticoid immunosuppression resulting in proliferation of harmful digestive bacteria (e.g., *Streptococcus bovis*) that have been implicated in the pathophysiology of laminitis.[1]

[1]Pollitt, Christopher (November 2003). "Equine Laminitis" (PDF). Proceedings of the AAEP, p. 49.

(Above) Near the base of the steep path leading to the upper track, the horses stop to "mine" roots and minerals from the earth. Here, Chakra, digs at the ground to expose the roots of an unidentified plant, whose top he will not eat. Horses instinctively and selectively know what, and what not, to eat — at least when given the opportunity of good choices.   *(Facing page)* Nearby, Chance licks at rocks he dug from the ground, delivering vital nutrients. Below him is a close-up of one of his front hooves — tough, sound, and perfectly shaped — and the gravelly earth that characterizes the entire track and which aids in the shaping of exemplary hooves on track. Zoo Paradise should provide similar footings for their ungulates, as well as comparable botanicals and mineral deposits that animal residents can harvest and mine on their own. It is thought, conventionally so, that such use of the hooves only serves to "wear away" their epidermal armor; to the contrary, it only serves to toughen the feet consistent with their ancient adaptation that "hooves are tools" to be used not coddled.

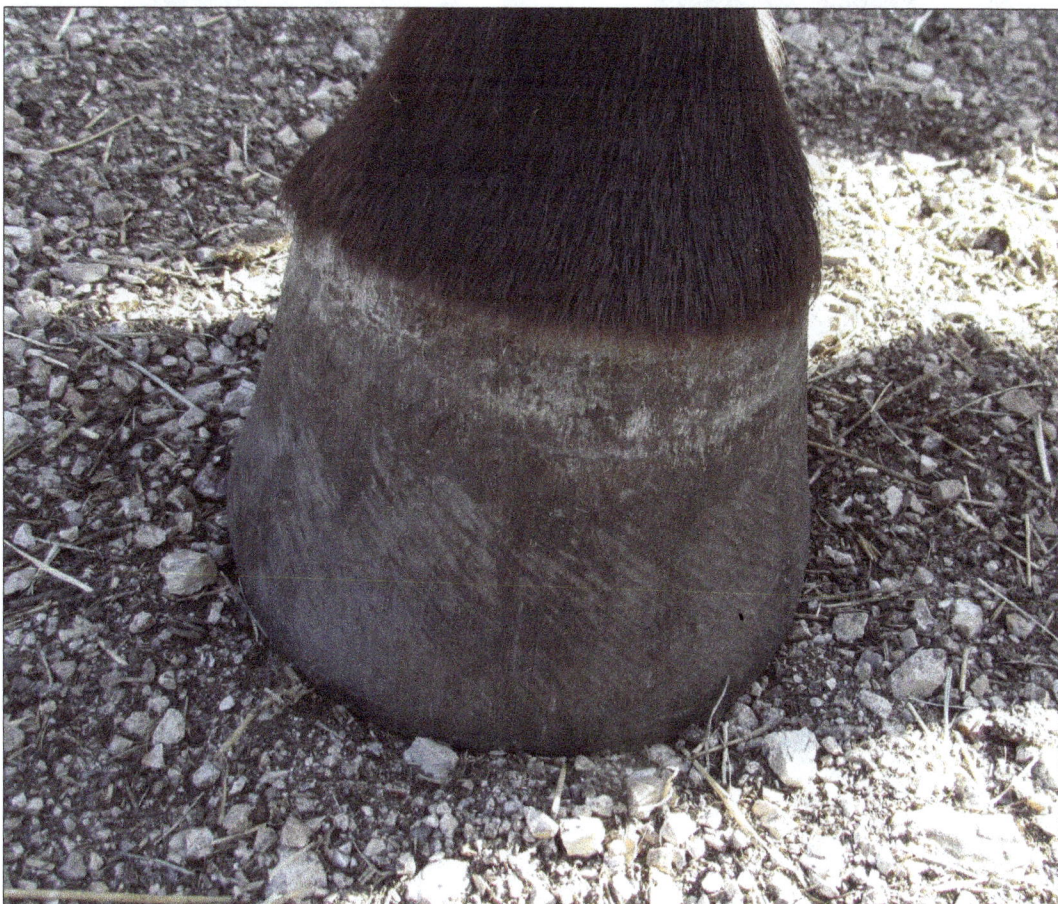

Our band must ascend a steep 200 foot change in elevation to reach the upper track loop. They do so in "formations" like this based on social hierarchy ("pecking order"), no different than what their species does in the wild. In Zoo Paradise, we should also facilitate species-based variations of these formations mediated by relative dominance.

Each horse has his own hay bag at each feed station, although sharing is more common than not. How much, and at what feed station, hay is consumed, provides important information on each horse's dietary habits and needs. We use half a dozen or more hay species to provide a variety of nutrients which also act probiotically on many ungulates to prevent digestive bacterial infections.

(Facing page) Adult male Somali (reticulated) giraffe feeding high-up on an acacia, in central Kenya. *(Above)* Giraffe bending down to drink. The circulatory system is adapted to deal with blood flow rushing down its neck. I have little doubt that our very successful feeding strategy — feeding "high and low" with netted bags — which mimics wild behavior, would work wonders, too, in Zoo Paradise for a range of species. As in Paddock Paradise, I see it not as a matter that animals — particularly those species with relatively long necks — *can* forage high and low, but that it is a biological *necessity* based on their adaptation to eat this way. From blood flow (circulation), to digestive processes and digestive juices, to organ function, to hoof shaping, to accessing a range of nutritious vegetation, a natural diet encompasses both food and how food is eaten.

Paddock Paradise takes advantage of biodiversity in many ways, including the availability of edible seasonal forages, not possible in any close confinement system as we see in zoos and even zoo paddocks.

(Above, left) Chakra and Audrey scale the hill leading from Feed Station #5 to #4 during late winter. At this time, the earth is relatively barren of any plant life on track or even the upper pasture. However, non-structural carbohydrates (NSCs) such as Fructan may still be highly concentrated in dormant pasture grasses even during winter, and, therefore, horses put in them to free-graze are at risk of laminitis. For this reason, horses living 24/7 on track and given a reasonably natural are not at risk.

(Above, right) View of the same stretch of track during spring. Forage is diverse and native on track in contrast to the conventional mono-cultured upper pasture on the other side of the electric fence. Even if NSC-rich plant life were present on the track, the amounts would be insufficient to saturate the horse's digestive system with sugars that eventually spawn laminitic episodes. This forage "safety net" inherent in Paddock Paradise works well with planned forages and supplements strategically positioned along the track, assuring that horses have enough of the right things to eat when they want and need it.

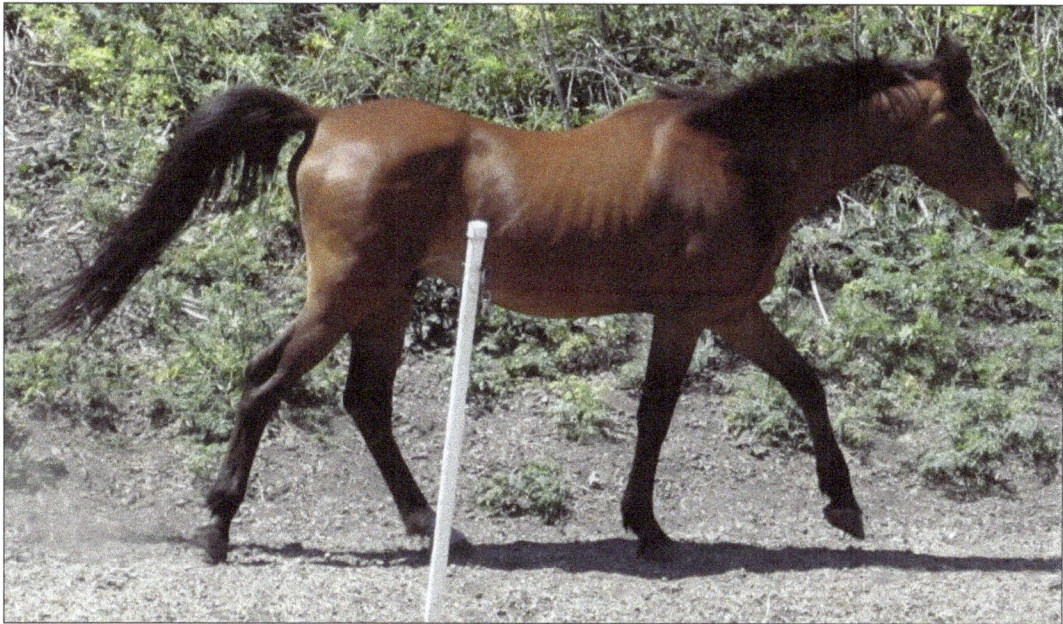

The seasonal changes that affect flora in Paddock Paradise also affect horses' *homeostasis* — the maintenance of relatively stable internal physiological conditions (e.g., body temperature and the pH of blood). This occurs through acclimation, a specialized form of adaptation, and is illustrated above with Apollo's very "furry" winter *(top)* and sparse summer *(bottom)* coats (outer covering of hair). Vitality through natural thermoregulation occurs precisely this way in wild horse country. Paddock Paradise facilitates this important biological mechanism, which, regrettably, is suppressed by many horse owners through the use of blankets and stalling their horses out of the elements. To the extent possible, the biological forces of homeostasis should also be facilitated with animals living in Zoo Paradise to serve their vitality.

Apollo and Chance arrive before the others at Feed Station #4. Stations #4 and #3 are where we usually put their favorite hays — as far away from their water source below as possible to promote maximum movement on track. Yet, "taste preferences" can change unpredictably overnight, and they will clean out their lesser favorite hay before returning to their clear favorite. Distant mountains peer towards the Pacific Ocean.

(Below) Once a week in early spring I bring out the Ranger UTV and "drag" the track to keep grass marginalized on the fence line and the inner pasture at bay altogether. In our tour of Zoo Paradise, you will see how the "inner" pasture track will transform to become the "people track".

Apollo has had his fill of whatever is at Feed Station #4 and is ascending the loop to "high point" at #3 to see what's available there. *Blue arrow* traces his direction. While Chakra nibbles away, Chance peers back at the "girls" of the tribe still down at #5. It is rare to see the band strung out on the track, particularly come night fall. In the wild, Apollo — an alpha — would take the rear and drive members forward — while his alpha mare would instinctively lead the way (it's in her DNA!). The social interplay between alpha (monarch) male and females is an extraordinary phenomenon of wild horse society, rarely seen in domestication. Paddock Paradise affords this opportunity. An opportunity to also accord many species in Zoo Paradise.

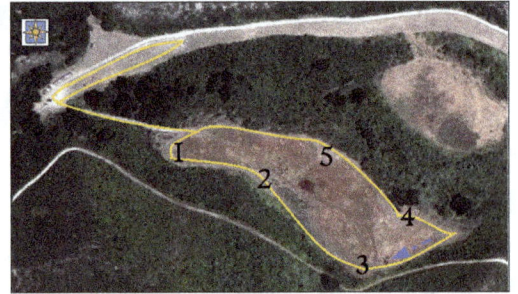

Moving along, Apollo (out of sight) has already taken his place at Feed Station #3, while the rest of the family band moves single file to catch up and take their respective places. In contrast to the lower track system near the water hole and rolling area, life up above is largely about testing and eating at each feed station. Given their digestive biology, this makes sense. With a steady flow of digestive acids, their species needs a steady intake of forage to prevent damage to their intestinal tract and to maintain the right balance of bacteria for good health. Feeding hay once or twice a day makes for hungry, angry horses — prone to ulcers. My observation at zoos tells me this problem is not just endemic to horses, but to many species whose natural eating behaviors are suppressed by human practices of "set meals" per day. Animals know when and what to eat — give the opportunity; hence, natural feeding behaviors *by species* is another fundamental pillar of Zoo Paradise.

(*Above*) The entire band has now reached the summit of the tracking system, Feed Station #3. To give this some perspective, the horses must ascend half a mile from the water trough to this point, a trek they will repeat more than once during the day. Wind at "high point" often gusts to 30 - 50 mph, and if an unknown or unwelcome scent or natural debris flying by puts the scare into them, they will gallop headlong in flight down the track for refuge. As a "stress" behavior, this type of exhilaration is beneficial to a prey species. The "track" based architecture of Paddock Paradise facilitates this behavior, and Zoo Paradise should follow suit. Further, pitting predator against prey adds yet another dimension of natural stress to the wilderness matrix that inures to vitality.

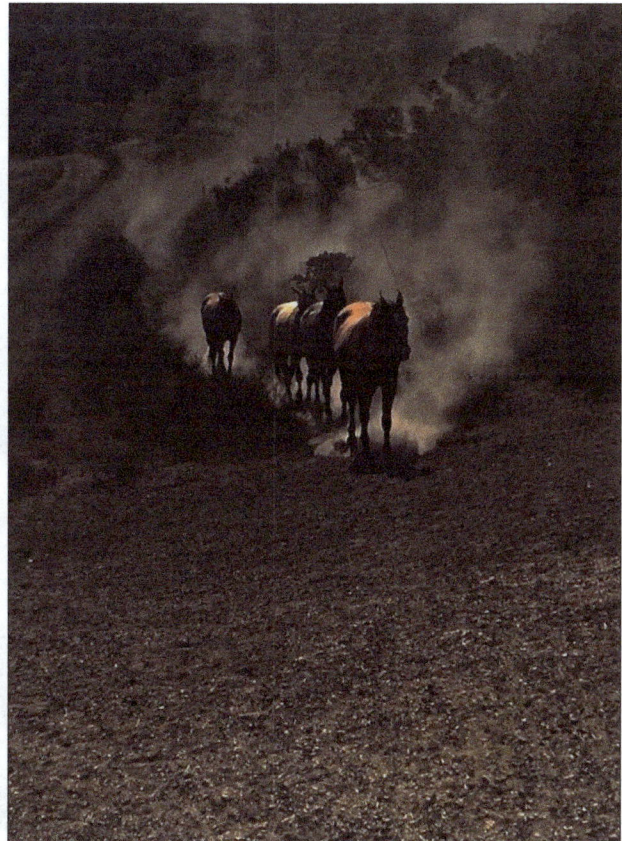

(*Above, left*) Chance gallops down the hill towards Feed Station #2 in response to some trigger; but falls obediently into his pecking order position at a walk once Apollo has determined there is no threat. The band quietly and orderly enters the feed station under Apollo's commanding authority.

In an attempt to "let nature" help stifle aggressive grass from entering the track by breeching the fence line, I begin to experiment with plant succession as a countermeasure:

(*Above, top*) The hillside just above Feed Station #2 had been completely denuded by the band's foraging habits the previous year. The entire area within and surrounding the hay poles was also devoid of any vegetation.

(*Above, bottom; facing page*) Since we do not seed the track with anything, I thought it would be interesting to see what came in the next year at this same seasonal juncture. Plant succession the following spring filled the hillside with new types of growth which the horses avoided eating. Dragging kept this new growth at bay from the feed station.

(*Above*) To my surprise, three new species of plant life succeeded the old hillside growth. Encroaching from the southern slope (*blue arrow*) came the yellow mustard; from the west side *hill (black arrow)* came a combination of thistle and yellow mustard; and last, on the flat coming from the north (*yellow arrow*) a creeping ground cover that releases a very horrible odor should I drag it. But nowhere did grass grow. Interesting was that none of these plant colonies entered the hay pole area and still remain at bay 3 months later.

(*Right*) Thistle and yellow mustard now came to dominate most of the fence line — but not the track itself — suppressing grass that was once dominant below the fence line while deterring the horses. I'm now able to turn off the electric fence.

We are nearing journey's end:

(Above) Visitors from the Netherlands are "escorted" by Chance (and the rest of the band) to Feed Station #1.

(Facing page, above) One last nibble before heading back down to the lower track.

(Facing page, below) Our band is arriving at the lower   track to see what's happening. What's about to happen is that I will be examining and trimming their hooves! As a farrier, horses would wisely run away from me, if given the chance, not liking one bit that I would be nailing steel to their hooves. But not in Paddock Paradise, where horses are never shod! Moreover, I turn the experience into a "treat festival", and always welcome visitors to watch and give the horses attention during breaks. The horses love this attention and eagerly line up to be trimmed, even threatening each other in hopes of reaching the front of the line. I make this point because it appears that Paddock Paradise, which mimics the species natural habitat, generally has the effect of improving relationships between horses and people. I don't see this in conventional equine boarding facilities, and it's no wonder if one simply views the species through the lens of nature. I predict that Zoo Paradise will have the same positive effect on its animals and visitors.

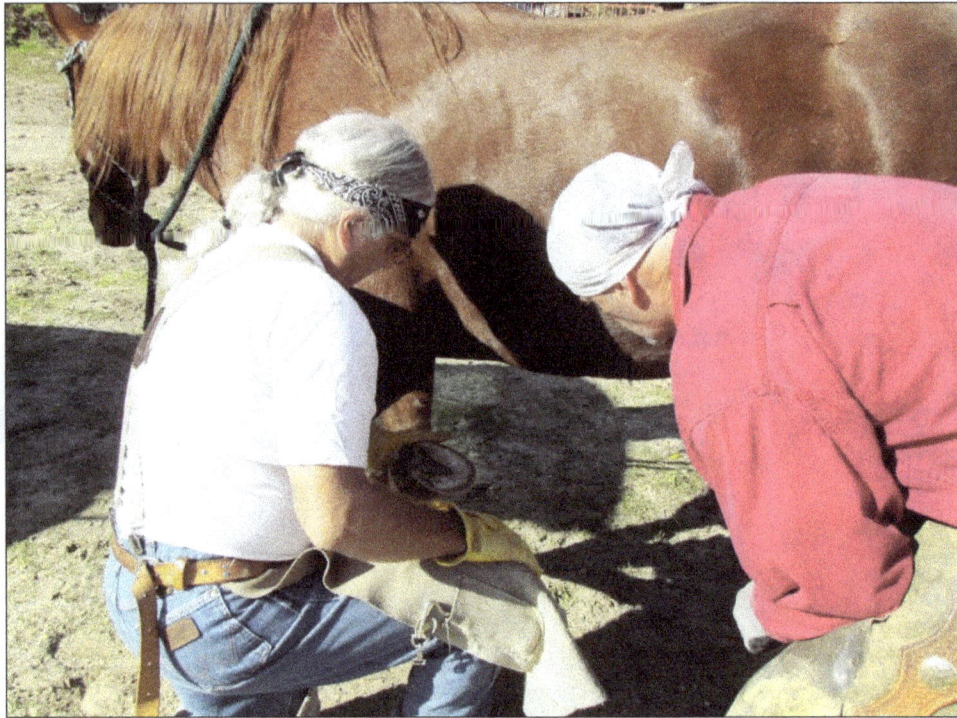

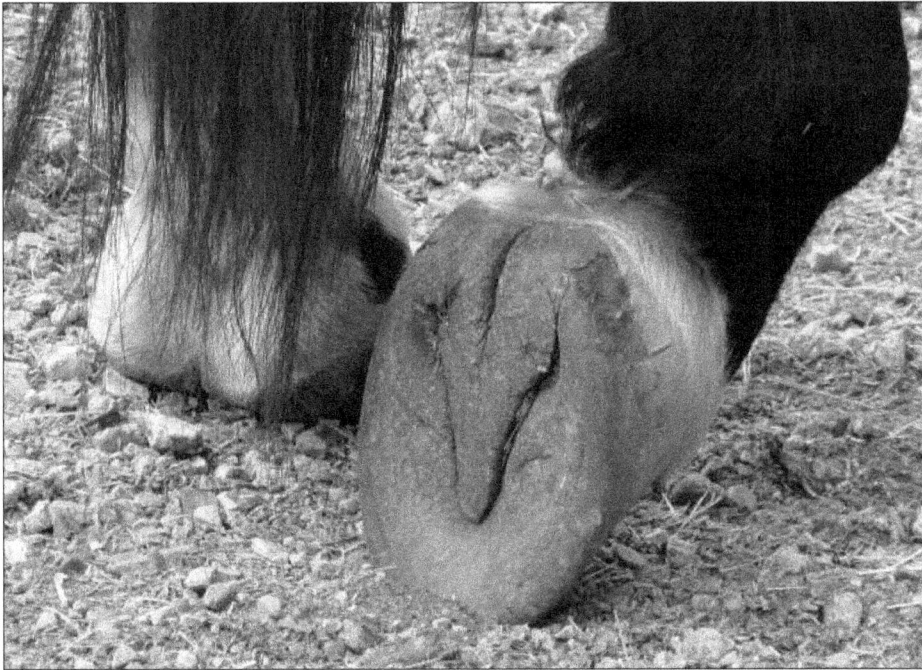

(Facing page, above) Natural hoof care practitioners evaluate a hoof in preparation for doing the natural trim. The science of natural hoof care is rooted deeply in the wild horse model. Years of academic and hands-on training are required to gain the knowledge and skills necessary to replicate the wild horse hoof.

(Facing page, below) Hind hoof trimmed in the "4th Position" according to natural trim guidelines and natural movements of the horse's limbs. The horse has been trained to what is called "sequencing", a comprehensive way to communicate with the horse through the equine language of "relative dominance", move safely and efficiently under the horse, and deploy tools and equipment in the most effective way possible to get the job done.

(This page) Close-up of exemplary naturally shaped hooves forged in Paddock Paradise.

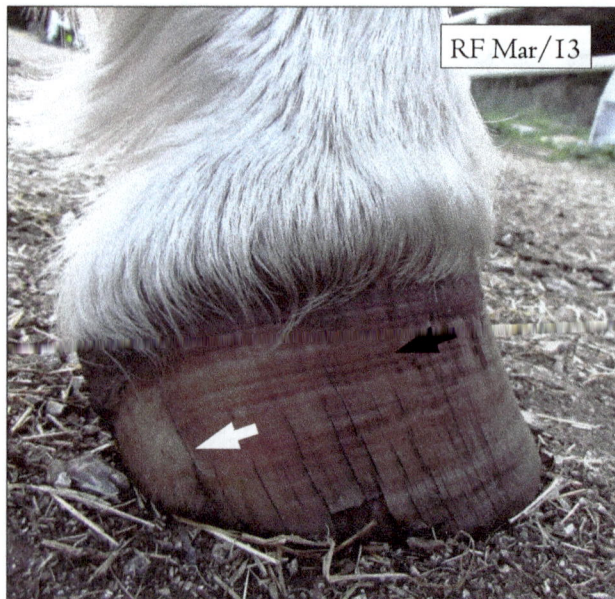

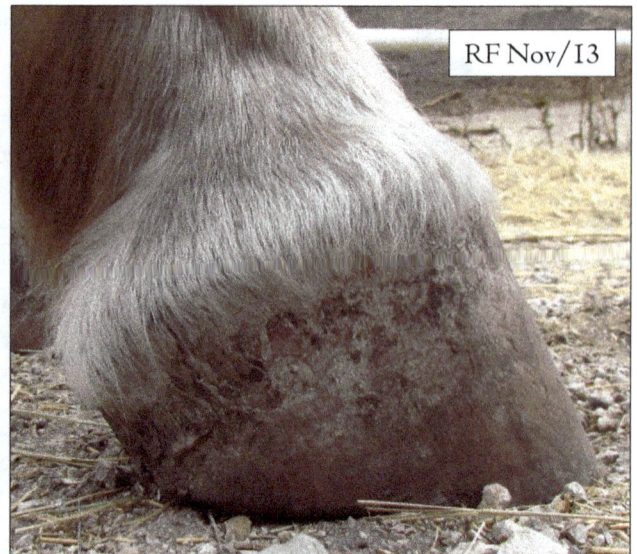

(*Above, left*) Band matriarch Audrey was brought to us with horrific hooves, deformed by chronic laminitis (Whole Horse Inflammatory Disease), numerous wall splits (some potentially very serious) and Navicular Syndrome (NS) — any traumatic, permanent damage done to the horse's body anywhere above the hoof resulting in chronic faltering. *Black arrow* points to one of many laminitis stress rings cascading down the hoof wall of her RF foot. Abnormally steep angle of growth proves to be a club foot, a characteristic of NS. *White arrow* points to a severe Quarter Crack, the result of unnatural wall stresses and/or coronet injuries.

(*Above, right*) Eight months after living on track the outer wall is nearly free of all stress rings, and Audrey is completely sound although the hoof is still confirmed to clubfoot. Her transformation, so far, suggests that NS may be healable in Paddock Paradise.

(*Facing Page*) Sampling of damaged hooves caused by unnatural horse and hoof care. The good news is that NHC, rooted in the laws of nature, not only will heal these tragedies, but will transfer to all species with hooves. My observations of hoof problems in zoos are revealing of either the same or similar problems seen here. In fact, even some wild game "reserves" set aside for displaced animals are often not habitat-appropriate based on the species adaptation. The example of a laminitic zebra hoof above reflects this clash between what conservationists see as habitat solutions versus what are the actual adaptive needs of a species that serve their vitality. But my intent here is not to publish an exposé of misguided care practices that I have witnessed or have been published by animal protection advocates, but merely to point us in a new direction. If you will, Zoo Paradise to the rescue!

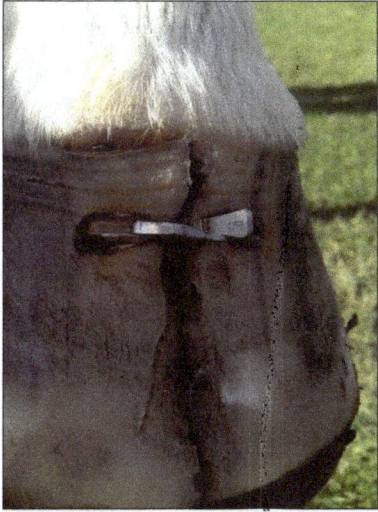
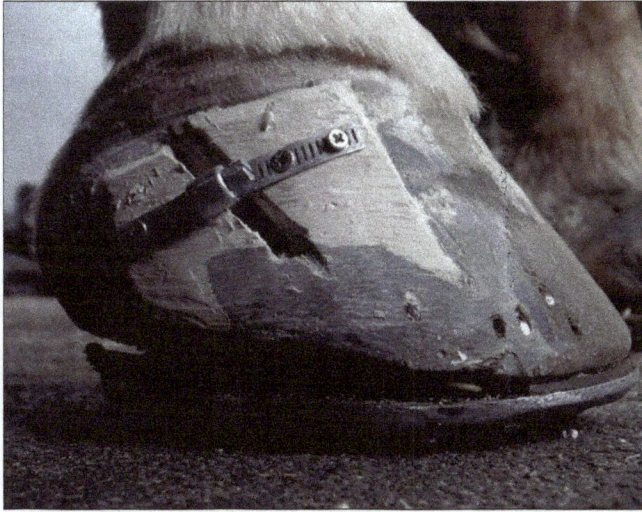

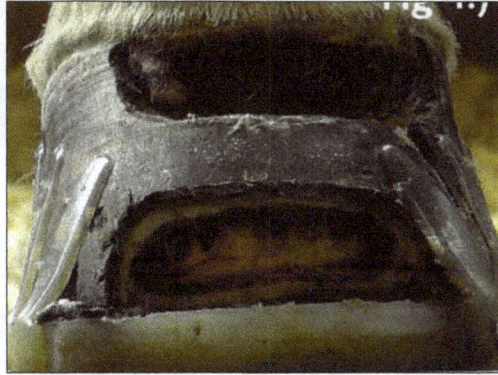
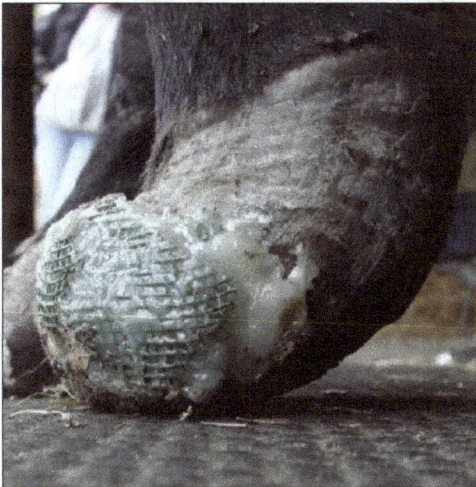
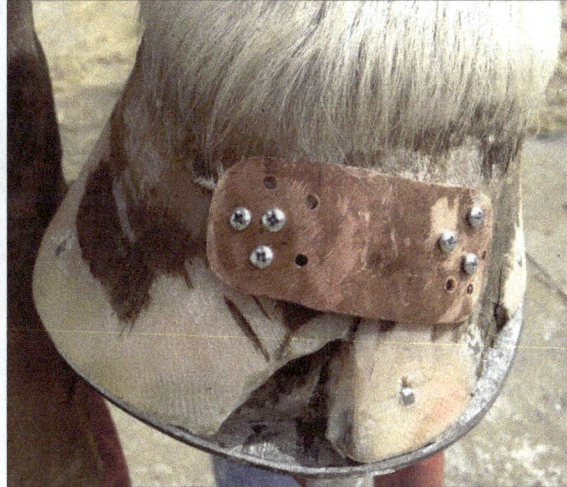

Summary

The purpose of this chapter was to open doors to another reality, a better reality, that we can create for wildlife held institutionally in captivity. Zoo Paradise, like Paddock Paradise, need not be relegated to the back burner as a useless concept. It is something we can, and should, make a reality.

Most horses today are still boarded based on what's convenient for the owner. The actual biological needs of the species are marginalized, if taken into consideration at all because their owners simply don't know what that means. But this is changing, as more and more horse owners worldwide become aware of, and pursue, genuinely humane natural boarding possibilities exemplified by Paddock Paradise. Zoo Paradise takes us down a similar path of awareness, recognizing that wild animals in today's zoos are shorn of their dignity, deprived of their biological needs, and segregated not only by species, but cleaved down to the isolated individual or compressed into ersatz herds with stolid faces and bizarre behaviors one never sees in their native homelands. In effect, they are housed liked horses.

The purpose of Zoo Paradise, as with Paddock Paradise, is to facilitate species specific habitats that encourage natural patterns of socialization. Our goal is to facilitate unobstructed movement through, in, and around a "tracking" network derived conceptually from the wild natural world. These tracks, speckled along the way with basic "things to do", have no other intent than to arouse the will in the animal to live and prosper with vitality. Paddock Paradise is existential proof that the concept is viable. Now, it's up to caring humans to bring the same vision and vital force to our zoological gardens (and wild game reserves!), to tear down their walls, and recreate them in the new paradigm given to us by the wild animals themselves.

To this end, I'll take the first step and set forth my own vision.

CHAPTER FOUR
Symbiosis

An important premise of all modern zoos today is to provide curious humans, whom we'll refer to as "visitors," the opportunity to observe and learn about captive wild animals, identified from here on as "residents." In this binary configuration, both visitors and residents in Zoo Paradise move in ways that facilitate the needs of each. Of course, administrators of Zoo Paradise shoulder the responsibility of making sure that the residents don't suffer for it! The *visitor* is curious and wants not only to see what the animals look like, but also how they behave, and in a structured environment that simulates the natural environment of their specie's native adaptation. On the other hand, *residents* have much to do to claim and sustain their vitality, which is facilitated by the "lessons from the wild" in an environment that is choreographed by park administrators — much as we have done for our horses living on track at the AANHCP Field Headquarters. For this to happen, Zoo Paradise, not surprisingly, must look somewhat different than either the Balboa Park or Wild Animal Safari zoo strains we see in every country today. However configured, the visitor must be able to observe without disturbing the resident, and residents must be able to traverse their home ranges according to the adaptive requirements of their respective species. Putting both of these objectives in our sights, the necessary paradigm shift leading us into Zoo Paradise will present itself.

Residents and Visitors

So, visitors have arrived now at Zoo Paradise to see and learn. We should accommodate them! At the same time, their quest must not interfere with the residents' survival chores elicited by the "lessons from the wild." Both are busy in their own ways. Visitors, further, must not be able to provoke the resident into "flinging his feces" at them, so to speak, so zoo administrators must be vigilant in their authority to keep the binary relationship in good order.[1] In my book, *Paddock Paradise*, I cautioned horse owners to construct their tracks such that human activity is minimal within them, and, as we've seen in the previous chapter, that the paths lead to locations (within the tracking system) where the "lessons from the wild" can be most propitiously positioned and brought to life. After all, Paddock Paradise is the home of the horse ("resident"), not the visitor, nor are the

---

[1]This concern applies equally to part employees, particularly those in close contact with the animals. This became an issue between myself and our horses in Paddock Paradise, wherein the horses became upset in how I managed their dung deposit through "dragging" with heavy equipment. Where and when, for example, horses relieve themselves has survival value in the wild, a matter I will take up later in this book since it could become a problem in Zoo Paradise too if we aren't vigilant in respecting their way of doing things. But my point here is that park employees and contractors constitute a special class of "visitors" in Zoo Paradise and, therefore, are not exempt from this discussion.

The 80-meter (260 ft) underwater tunnel in Aquarium Barcelona. The designers are on the right path, but the fish are still caged. Fish migrate in the ocean and in rivers, thus they too need their paths, not just the humans as depicted here.

residents' tracks the playground of the visitor — they are, once more, the resident's *home*. Visitors, hence, are temporary guests, not residents. Thus, an important dimension of the paradigm shift is that there are two worlds in Zoo Paradise, and above all, their binary relationship must be respected, defended, and enforced to the greatest degree possible by zoo administrators. When human intrusion is not kept in check, the scales of balance tip in favor of the current conundrum facing modern zoological gardens, and the very fabric of Zoo Paradise threatens to unravel.

Visitors to Zoo Paradise must have their own safe haven — visitor tracks, in fact — amid all the wild residents. I believe this will be straight forward to do, and I will depict proposed examples in the next chapter. As they traverse Zoo Paradise, visitors should be provided with important educational opportunities. Wild animals and their environments are, as I mentioned earlier, under siege due to the intrusions of humans who want their land base and its resources. Thus, explications concerning the plight of wildlife outside Zoo Paradise, and what visitors can do to help, should integrate with any discussion of resident behavior within Zoo Paradise. In this way, Zoo Paradise can serve the residents in the broadest sense of their survival as a species, far beyond their tracks within Zoo Paradise, especially those facing eminent extinction.

Residents of Zoo Paradise know what to do with their lives, we simply have to af-

Sable antelope in zoo. On another occasion at the San Diego Zoo, a lone young male gazelle (antelope) was looking longingly and apprehensively towards a wall, on the other side of which was a small band of females in their own enclosure. As I was photographing him, visitors to my side queried the obvious, "Why don't they have him with the others so he'll be happy?" A good question. This youngster's desire to be with his own species — they are herd animals — actually puts him at the center of an ongoing heated debate. The purported necessity of putting males in solitary confinement because they may try to breed females. While the turbulent politics of population control through irreversible sterilization and problematic chemical contraceptives rages among conflicting factions of wildlife advocates, scientists, government regulators, and others, configuring animals on track in Zoo Paradise according to relative dominance may open new doors to regulating fertility naturally that are acceptable on all sides.

ford them the opportunity *to act*. This will require the tight coordination of zoologists, biologists, and others most familiar with each resident species in the planning and construction of Zoo Paradise. My personal expertise is limited to horses, so, beyond my vision and experience with Paddock Paradise as a foundational model that works, someone like myself wouldn't be qualified to say much of anything with the possible exception of the resident zebras! Which is to say that the creation of Zoo Paradise with respect to the residents life styles will require the participation of experts knowledgeable of species in the native habitats, not just anyone!

Residents vis-à-vis residents

Leaving the world of the visitor in Zoo Paradise, we now turn our attention to the symbiotic relationships among its residents. The core idea here is, when possible, to integrate species whose lives would have been so melded in the wild. The reason for doing this is to inspire natural behaviors, from which natural movement is derived, which in

Hippo wading pool at a zoo — not exactly "anything is better than nothing," because the effort couldn't be more perfunctory! Back at the San Diego Zoo, I discovered that engineers there clearly went to great lengths to create a hippo pool that could only suggest simulation of a wild watering hole to those who don't know any better. If biologists were on the job, they were clearly asleep. The youngster submerged in the pool, like the antelope on the facing page, was alone — and his isolation and obvious depression didn't go unnoticed by me and other visitors. Above the noisy din of park tractors and bitch barkers on park tour buses, visitors, who truly were excited by the prospect of seeing a real live hippo, rose discernable voices of frustration and anger at the spectacle. I held my own tongue, but took note as I laid the groundwork for this book.

turn propels the animals along their paths in Zoo Paradise. This behavior based conduit is what will deliver the energy forces of vitality to each and every animal.

Prey-predator forces

A primal force operative at all times in nature is that of predation. To live, one must eat, and to eat one must secure prey. Thus, how prey and predator live in relation to each other in the wild, is not only a critical element of each animal's vitality, but an important consideration in the planning and construction of Zoo Paradise. We have seen that the threat of cougar (mountain lion) predation is a constant presence in the minds of our horses living at the AANHCP Field Headquarters; in fact, this "pressure" is there whether or not a cougar is anywhere nearby. I wrote in my sixth book, *The Natural Trim: Principles and Practice*, how this prey-predator tension served to shape the hooves naturally for the rigors of life in the wild:

> There are many social behaviors that, from the standpoint of movement, contribute to the shaping of his hoof in the wild. But there is a less conspicuous force that drives all of these behaviors. This is his innate "prey awareness" rooted deeply in his specie's biology and evolutionary history; in

fact, the horse is an animal of prey, something he is intensely aware of at all times. This is to say it is genetically encoded within his DNA and in his perceptions of the world around him. This is true whether he is living in the wild or isolated with humans in domestication. As such, he instinctively senses that he is vulnerable to predators if he cannot move soundly [with] unrestricted freedom to move. We see this same prey awareness in other wild ungulates such as the zebra, gazelle, and deer. This keen awareness also keeps him mentally and physically fit and "on alert" at all times — rendering him, in the wild, a limber equine athlete as a consequence. Hence, the import and importance of prey psychology into the shaping of his hooves cannot be ignored or underestimated.[1]

Zoo administrators, therefore, should find ways to intertwine the species, pitting predator against prey, generating a tension that serves both specie's vitality. This could happen on two levels: simulated only to facilitate extraordinary movement, and, as a survival means to an end, as it occurs in the wild. Organized appropriately in conjunction with relative dominance and on-track breeding, predation could also serve to temper or balance fecundity. I would add, further, that predation should be an important educational experience, perhaps selectively so, for human visitors.

Centripetal and centrifugal RD forces in family units

Family units lie at the foundation of most animal societies, and within these structures lie the centripetal and centrifugal forces of relative dominance (RD). In the horse's natural world, for example, RD is a centripetal force used by the horse to define his space relative to others in his specie's hierarchical social order ("pecking order"). RD is countered by a centrifugal force — his instinct as an animal of prey to be part of a herd, specifically the family or "band" unit. These contraposing forces are best understood in terms of what biologists call the "sphere of intolerance" (*facing page*).

The sphere of intolerance is a measure of a horse's relative comfort or discomfort with those around him. This may be a fellow family member, or another intrusive species. Accordingly, the sphere contracts or relaxes corresponding to pressure applied to or removed from it. For example, aggression by one horse towards another affects each horse's sphere. If sufficient pressure is applied, the sphere of the less dominant horse contracts and he will move away from his more dominant adversary. This "driving" force is the *centripetal force* of RD (which also plays an important role when I am working with a horse to trim his hooves and cooperation is needed).

A countering *centrifugal force* lies in the herd instinct, embedded deep within each individual's sphere of intolerance. The herd instinct acts as a strong nuclear force to draw horses together for their survival, and, accordingly, their sphere's relax as members move

[1] *The Natural Trim*, p. 65.

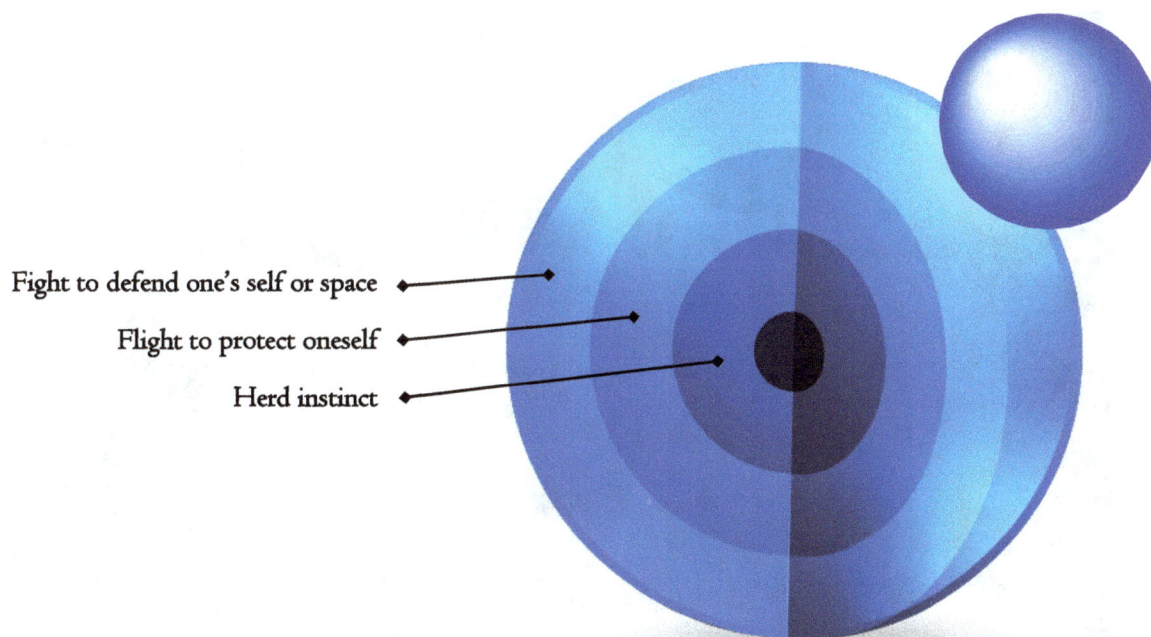

Fight to defend one's self or space ◆—
Flight to protect oneself ◆—
Herd instinct ◆—

(Above) Relative dominance (RD) in relation to the horse's sphere of intolerance. The sphere, a measure of a horse's relative comfort as he interacts with other family members, either shrinks or contracts depending on with whom he is interacting at the moment. Contraction also drives the individual towards the protective embrace of the family unit when faced by external threats. *(Left)* Aggression by one dominant member contracts the sphere of a more beta member, resulting in flight ("Get away from me!"). This is expected normal and healthy behavior among and between many species, and life on track in Zoo Paradise will provide visitors with many displays of exciting interactions worth writing home about!

willingly into close proximity. Hence, the basic social unit of equine life in the wild — the family band — counters the strong centrifugal force that protects the individual. From birth to death, each horse's sphere lies in tension with others' in the family unit, contracting and relaxing as interactions dictate. And within this social constraint, each horse is able to act out to their fullest what it means to be a highly motivated and instinctual animal whose constitution is imbued with vitality.

Adolescent male bulls sparring.

Male sexual competition

Male sexual competition, such as stallion rivalry among wild horses; lekking among insects, birds, and amphibians; rut among ruminants (e.g., deer, elk, and antelope); and possibly musth among bull elephants,[1] is another key force that can and should be facilitated in Zoo Paradise. The presence of a monarch breeding male not only serves the sexual forces of natural selection, it enables subordinate (beta) non-breeding males to take their place on track without the necessity of sterilization. Since integrating breeding males in any domestic environment with females and other non-sterilized males is commonly discouraged as problematic — with the possible exception of breeding operations — further discussion here is merited if the idea is to be even considered in Zoo Paradise.

It is well-known that a specie's adaptative environment favors fecundity — the signature of a successful adaptation as a result of natural selection.[2] Because the tracking system of Zoo Paradise simulates that native environment, the potential for successful breeding is optimized in accordance with the laws of natural selection. This potential

[1]Musth or "must" is a periodic state of the bull elephant characterized by aggressive behavior usually connected with the rutting season and dominance. Cases of elephants chasing giraffes, and killing rhinoceroses without provocation in national parks in Africa have been documented and are attributed to musth in young male elephants. Studies show that reintroducing older males into an elephant population seems to prevent younger males from entering musth, stopping this aggressive behavior. Bearing this in mind, old and young bull elephants should both be present together in Zoo Paradise. See: "Killing of black and white rhinoceroses by African elephants in Hluhluwe-Umfolozi Park, South Africa" by Rob Slotow, Dave Balfour, and Owen Howison. *Pachyderm 31* (July–December, 2001):14–20. Accessed 14 September 2007.
[2]*The Natural Horse*, p. 9, for a discussion of America's prolific wild, free-roaming horses.

Turtles sparring at a national park in Ramat Gan, Israel.

particularly has far reaching implications for those animals removed from the wild facing the threat of extinction, and for whom natural — rather than compulsory or artificial — breeding in captivity is of paramount importance. In fact, sexual competition simply favors the sustainability of healthy zoo populations under any circumstance, and it seems to me that this should be an ongoing concern of all zoo breeding regimes.

I believe the attitude underlying habitat policies that exclude or discourage non-breeding, unsterilized males from participating in mixed male-female domestic populations stems directly from a misunderstanding of the social dynamics of relative dominance (RD) as it would occur in the wild. This follows from misguided observations, baseless assumptions about what is natural, and erroneous conclusions drawn from RD behavior among domesticated breeding males living within unnatural herd configurations and, typically, unnatural living conditions too. Inversions (discussed in Chapter 2) at the AANHCP Field Headquarters are an example, wherein male monarch alphas may behave like alpha females in the absence of stallion rivalry. The preclusion of male bachelor bands — usually through castration — is another example, wherein the hormonal effects of testosterone are removed and males then assume beta female positions in the herd's pecking order. The assumption that all stallions are "born" alpha monarchs destined to breed is yet another example; in fact, one more rationale for castration and the suppression bachelor bands. Each of these contrives to obstruct natural selection and favor "line breeding" (inbreeding). Because Zoo Paradise simulates the wild (adaptive) environ-

Wild horse bands mingle with range cattle at southwestern Nevada water hole.

ment, it is imperative that those attitudes be challenged and not allowed to prevail when they are clearly unjustified. In the wild, natural selection favors breeding by the monarch alpha male, a role he assumes by driving any competitor away from his mate (or harem) and into a bachelor band or by subordinating him to an allied extended family social unit, wherein he may breed too. Each species has its own telos — a defined "way" of providing all males a place within the embrace of a family type unit, nuclear or remote (bachelor bands), thereby creating a future "pool" of potential breeders to assure variation and survival of the species. Indeed, surely nature, after millions of years of evolution, did not err in using male sexual competition as a principal force to assure thriving populations. Nor should we.

Resident vis-à-vis Flora

Many of today's zoological gardens are, for all practical purposes, botanical masterpieces as well. I've referenced the San Diego Zoo's splendid landscapes, which truly rival — actually, surpass — the animal enclosures in capturing the essence of wildness. But if we look at matters from the standpoint of the residents, the landscape is actually pretty monotonous. Unlike visitors, who get to go nearly anywhere they please, the residents are stuck, held hostage to a single location, day in, day out, year after year. That's all they get to see — and they can't touch any of it either. Furthermore, while some may be able to hear animals elsewhere, most never see each other, and certainly there isn't any physical contact. The only interaction is with gawking and noisy visitors, and whoever feeds or cleans their cages after hours. Needless to say, the tracking system of Zoo Paradise will change all of that. And the sooner the better!

Zoo administrators will have to call upon a range of botanists with expertise in the adaptive environments from which the animals came. Artists, landscapers and various engineers will put that knowledge to work in designing and laying out the tracking system. Of that, I'm not worried — they can do a great job. What worries me is what the animals are going to eat, and how they're going to eat it. If it can be part of the landscape in some measure, as in the wild, all the better. What I am raising as a central issue is "diet" and "feeding behavior", together possibly the most critical cornerstone of Zoo Paradise.

Feeding the residents

Zoo Paradise means naturalizing the resident's entire life style, including what and how he eats. Ideally, his food should be what he eats in the wilds of his adaptive environment, a virtual guarantee of vitality. But, as I was reminded by my recent visit to the San Diego Zoo, the residents were fed pretty much like domesticated horses, swine, and cattle: pelleted commercial feeds and hay. Increasingly, such feeds are becoming laced with sugars (e.g., molasses and beet pulp), rice bran, and chemical contaminants that seem to go hand-and-glove with the industrialization of the food chain. Not surprisingly, the rise of obesity, insulin resistance, foot diseases, and other metabolic disorders in these animals seems to be paralleling the growing numbers of people with diabetes. I can personally testify to the near epidemic levels of laminitis (inflammation of the foot's "hoof-to-horse" dermal attachment mechanism) in horses around the world. All in all, we're talking about unnatural feeds being given to animals that their native digestive systems did not evolve to process. But that's not all!

How animals are fed can be an equally serious problem. In the wild, horses are actually nibblers, light foragers who nibble at this and that as the move along, day and night. Back in domestication, they are fed one, two, or, if "lucky", three "set meals" per day — like people. But they are not people, and their digestive systems are not designed nor equipped to eat like humans. One consequence, and a serious one since it is the number one killer of horses, is colic (severe gastrointestinal distress). *Paddock Paradise* was written in large part to help horse owners get their horses into more natural feeding regimens, as discussed in the previous chapter. We can do similar things in Zoo Paradise, providing each species reasonably natural diets and positioning their edibles along the track in ways

that simulate their adaptative environments. I found this challenge both exciting and its success rewarding at our AANHCP Field Headquarters, and marvel at the many wonderful ideas horse owners come up with around the world. I'm sure that progressive zoo administrators and their armies of talented scientists, engineers and care providers will enthusiastically take up the challenge too and create wonders that visitors and residents alike will enjoy. I have a few ideas of my own for Zoo Paradise!

Summary

Not surprisingly, symbiosis in Zoo Paradise is complex and predicated on a unique tension between visitors and residents as well as among the residents themselves. Of the former, visitors, anxious to observe and learn from the wild residents, must conduct themselves in new ways that respect and facilitate their vitality. The "old zoo" paradigm with its meandering paved passageways full of non-stop noisy visitors gawking at caged animals will not work, serving only to vanquish the very spirit of wildness sought by the visitors and needed by the residents. Of the latter, the centripetal forces of familial and herd bonds must give and take with the centrifugal forces of relative dominance and the symbiotic needs of those residents who would prey upon them. Within this complex matrix of interrelated species zoo administrators must flesh out the educational opportunities owed the visitors while delivering the broad spectrum of behavioral stimuli — from diet to locomotion — deserved of the residents.

But, as in Paddock Paradise, there are certain ground rules we must all acknowledge and abide by if this unprecedented symbiosis is to work unequivocally for all parties involved. These, not surprisingly, are the "lessons from the wild" that dwell within each wild species. The vision of Zoo Paradise provides us with the perfect dynamic foundation for these lessons to unfold. And to this end, the time to apply them has arrived.

CHAPTER FOUR
Welcome to Zoo Paradise!

An important premise of Zoo Paradise is its adaptability to a broad range of terrains and climates. How it conforms to the land will depend largely on which species of wild animals will be residents there and what their adaptive requirements are. The size, shape and location of the land must correlate to how it will be used, who the residents will be and in what numbers according to their species. As in Paddock Paradise, vitality in Zoo Paradise will hinge upon meeting the residents basic needs — principally diet, socialization (including prey-predator symbiosis), and freedom to move 24/7.

The types of "lessons from the wild" discussed previously in this book in relation to Paddock Paradise provide us with the essential guidelines for constructing Zoo Paradise. The lessons are those things that animals living in their wild adaptive environments do, day in and day out, to sustain their vitality. Our challenge is to provide a living space that inspires and facilitates those activities. The purpose of the lessons is to elicit behavioral responses — summarized in the chart at right (*facing page*) — that cause the animals to move naturally. Which is to say, it is not enough that the animals just move, *they must move naturally and diversely so in accordance with the behavioral responses elicited by the lessons from the wild.*

Biologists who have studied our residents in the wild are the experts who will be best equipped to cross link these lessons, species by species, to the behavioral responses we are seeking in Zoo Paradise. If we are negligent or slack in facilitating these lessons, we will be stuck with expensive veterinary (and hoof care) bills and listless, miserable animals — certainly by optimal wildlife standards. So, to keep our residents moving forward naturally with vitality, the lessons must be applied diligently and consistently. As a pragmatist, I also look at it this way: the more faithfully we apply the lessons, the less work and money we have to expend to keep residents healthy. And it also goes without saying that Zoo Paradise will make an indelible impression upon visitors, inculcating them with an invaluable understanding of wildlife, habitat, behavior, and symbiosis. Something they will want to support.

We recall from this book's preface that wildlife activists and others are working hard to save wildlife in their native lands. Once more, Zoo Paradise could be a powerful tool to gain the public's support by making them aware of what animals truly need to be healthy — certainly not cages and empty pastures with nothing to do — or native lands ravaged by civil wars, corporate raiders, and outlaw ivory hunters.

"Lessons from the Wild" Stimuli for Natural Behavior and Movement				
Lesson		*Description*		*Type*
Agonistic		Alert, alarm, and flight; aggression; stallion inter-actions; influence of rank order on daily activity.		Extraordinary
Comfort		Self-indulgent (sunning, shelter-seeking, licking, nibbling, scratching, rubbing, rolling, shaking and skin twitching, tail switching); mutual interactions (mutual grooming and symbiotic relationship. with birds).		Ordinary
Communicative		Visual expressions, acoustical expressions, squeal, nickers, whinny, groan, blow, snort, snore, other sounds, tactile interactions, chemical (pheromonal) exchanges.		Extraordinary Ordinary
Coprophagous		Consumption of dung.		Unusual
Dominance		Pecking order and alliances.		Extraordinary
Eliminative		Urinating and defecating.		Ordinary
Ingestive		Feeding, drinking, nursing.		Ordinary
Investigative		Curiosity.		Extraordinary Ordinary
Ontogeny		Perinatal and postnatal.		Extraordinary Ordinary
Play		Solitary, parent/young, sibling, younger/older.		Extraordinary
Reproductive		Sexual (male/female) and paternal/maternal.		Extraordinary Ordinary
Resting		Standing and recumbency.		Ordinary
Sleep		Recumbency.		Ordinary
Rogue		Partially or mainly solitary		Ordinary Extraordinary
Social Group		Herd and band structure, migratory, roles.		Extraordinary Ordinary
Social Pair Bonding		Adult/offspring, peer, heterosexual, paternal, interspecies.		Extraordinary Ordinary
Territorial		Home range and territoriality		Ordinary

The tracking system for Zoo Paradise will parallel that of Paddock Paradise (for equines) in many respects, but will require "multi-tracking" to accommodate a range of species that would otherwise not naturally or safely integrate. So, in each instance, on each track, the lessons from the wild must be facilitated with equal attention to detail according to species. And amid these tracks, visitors must also be accommodated! Let's discuss what that means now, borrowing an oxymoron used as a chapter sub-heading in my book Paddock Paradise . . . .

No Humans Allowed!

Zoo Paradise is the residents' home, or more precisely, their *home ranges*. I believe we should respect it as such, and, for the most part, stay out of it. This is the way wild animals prefer it in their native haunts, and what is natural for them should apply equally, or nearly so, to their wild brethren now living in captivity. After all, Zoo Paradise's residents don't intrude in your home, do they?

There are actually other important reasons for the "no humans allowed" clause of Zoo Paradise. Foremost, we are trying to simulate a wild animal environment in which multiple interacting species can prosper. Turning their world into a human playground — typical of zoos today, including the many "petting zoos" which facilitate commingling of humans with animals — only serves to undermine a vital premise of Zoo Paradise. Within Zoo Paradise, we strive to create natural conditions for the residents. That which we create for them is carefully calculated to elicit behavioral responses, which, in turn, catalyze natural behavior-based movement on track. Accordingly, we should make every effort to minimize our many possible human influences, while maximizing the scents, sounds and socialization patterns of the wilderness animal lifestyle. We can accomplish this by integrating our own interesting visitor tracks throughout Zoo Paradise that neither disturb nor obstruct those of the residents.

Creating the tracks!

The "tracks" are the "arteries" of Zoo Paradise, and the many "lessons" positioned strategically within its circuitry will constitute its vital nervous system. The tracks are the main passageways along which we seek to propel the residents forward naturally with impulsion and vitality — precisely the opposite of the boxed-in prisoners, whose sleep-mope-sleep indifference is speckled nearly everywhere with neurotic behaviors in zoos today. Putting the residents "on track" with appropriate stimulation, thus, is a principal objective.

In the wild, myriad paths weave their way through the home ranges, some shared, some not. But in all instances, each species is "glued" by instinct to move forward upon these paths, driven by their survival instincts elicited by the same "lessons from the wild" we will shower upon the residents of Zoo Paradise. For this reason, survival, administered through the "lessons," are serious business in Zoo Paradise, just as they are in the wild. We will find that all wild animals in Zoo Paradise share the same common will to survive that their species do in the wild. It is the same will that keeps them habitually "on track" in Zoo Paradise, for they crave order and familiarity as they negotiate their environment to find the things they need to live and prosper with vitality. Anything which threatens to jar them off their course or deprive them of their natural resources and socialization patterns, therefore, is perceived by them as a direct threat to their survival. In short, they will cling to the track that meets their needs with the same unrelenting tenacity and force that holds metal filings to a magnet. Zoo Paradise serves this primal magnetism by putting them "on track" — a living allegory of their ancient adaptation — and sustaining them there for their own good with things to do that serve their specie's vitality — and maybe ours too!

The illustration (and please forgive its rudimentary artistry — I'm not an artist) on the *overleaf* provides a simple diagrammatic template for a network of tracks that will accommodate many large and small resident prey species that are herbivorous and herd-oriented, including such ungulates as antelope, zebras, elephants, and giraffes. Predator residents, such as lions, will be strategically positioned along and in close proximity of the track, as well as water dwelling residents such as hippos and crocodiles. Residents such as gorillas and mountain sheep will occupy more limited home ranges that will suit their species. Obviously, in terms of biome possibilities, no two Zoo Paradises need be the same. So I will leave it to biologists and engineers to expand or contract this template to facilitate appropriate multi-track systems based on climate, land availability, numbers of animals in their system, and which species will be residents in them. Human ingenuity knows no boundaries, and Zoo Paradise — still uncharted territory — will demand much creative thinking and innovativeness from us. So, this is simply one concept based on the central theme of delivering vitality to all of our residents, and an interesting and education experience for our visitors.

Let's take a tour of Zoo Paradise!

The remainder of this chapter represents my own interpretation of the template in the *overleaf*. It is a visionary "tour" of sorts, describing what representative animals might be doing in a Zoo Paradise. Of course, no such place exists yet, so I've had to use my imagination for the most part, while drawing also upon my experiences in wild horse country and in Paddock Paradise, and here and there incorporating the useful observations, images, and biometrics provided by biologists and others who have studied the

Overleaf:
"Welcome to
Zoo Paradise"

Welcome to Zoo Paradise

Gorilla Mtn.

gorilla mountain

Paradise Falls

#1

#2

Big River

Falls Creek

large herbivore track

visitor track

N
W E
S

#3

#4

Rain Forest Creek

#6

Creek

Western Savannah

Falls

Flamingo Island

#5

Western Observation Platform

Big

River

Central Observation Platform

#12

#11

Bison & wild horse track

Great Basin

Western Jungle

#7

#10

1st crossing

Odyssey

rapids

2nd crossing

Rain Forest Café

#8

Rain Forest

Lagoon

High Peak

#9

visitor track

large herbivore track

Southern Alps

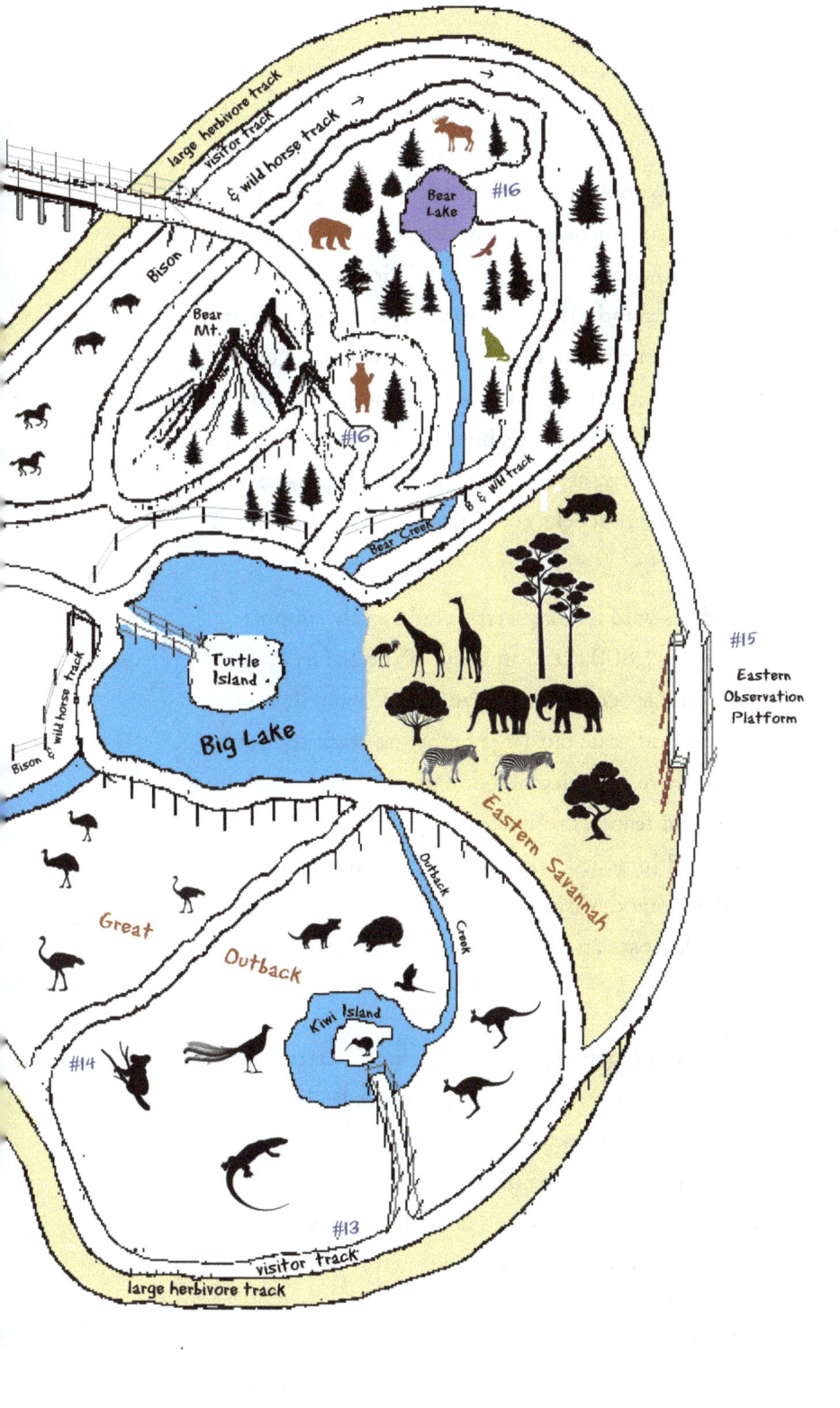

Zoo Paradise Key

Large herbivore track

Lakes, lagoon, river, and creeks

large herbivore track

visitor track

& wild horse track

Bison

Bear Mt.

Bear Lake

#16

#16

Bear Creek

B & wh track

Turtle Island

Big Lake

wild horse track

Bison & wild horse track

#15

Eastern Observation Platform

Eastern Savannah

Outback Creek

Great Outback

Kiwi Island

#14

#13

visitor track

large herbivore track

many species involved. While admittedly quite the challenge, the tour has also been quite fun in putting it together, an adventure "in wonderland!" If I seem to be taking liberties or reaching too far, why not? We can think big, small, or not at all. I prefer to push the envelop, and beckon others to do the same!

The featured land and waterway tracks in our tour weave in a serpentine manner intersecting at numerous junctions across Zoo Paradise. Large walls form the periphery of Zoo Paradise, beyond which lies "civilization." What those walls will look like invites much discussion, but my thinking is that they should serve as a shield and a buffer from the "outer world" of civilization, and as an inconspicuous warehouse for supporting technology. The only major and visible opening to the outer world is the "Grand Visitors Entrance." But once visitors leave its staging grounds, they become, for the most part, invisible sightseers in Zoo Paradise: largely unseen and unheard by our residents. I would also include park workers in this restriction. I recall from my recent zoo visits that the competition for making noise between visitors and the park's hot dog stands, cafes, curio shops, trams, buses and jitneys, carpenters, jack hammers, tractors, and loud speakers was fierce — only the screeching of the free-ranging peacocks could rise above the man-made din.

The land base commonly used in today's wild animal safaris could easily support multi-tracks five to ten miles long, such as the 1,800 acre San Diego Wild Safari Park. Even the 100 acre San Diego Zoo at Balboa Park could transform into a two mile system. In our Zoo Paradise, we'll compromise and scale our large herbivore track to four miles in length. As I've said above, because there is no actual Zoo Paradise yet, I'm taking a few liberties in giving our track some special features to make it interesting for both residents and visitors alike. If Disneyland and Jurassic Park can do it, why not Zoo Paradise? We'll begin our adventure tour at the "Grand Visitors Entrance" to Zoo Paradise, where visitors may arrive daily at 8 am (park closes an hour before sundown).

Grand Visitors Entrance

Park engineers have spared no expense nor ingenuity in constructing an extraordinary staging area from which visitors may head off on an array of pathways leading into the principal sectors of Zoo Paradise. From any of these, one can venture into the various "veins" — micro "paradises" that suit the biological needs of the park's diverse species. Adding to the initial excitement of new visitors, Zoo Paradise's large herbivores — elephants, rhinos, zebras, antelopes, and more — move along the "large herbivore track" (*light yellow path*) that circumscribes the entire park. This track lies directly beneath the "bridges" emanating like spokes from the visitor staging area, providing potentially extraordinary bird's-eye views of our residents on the move below — if timing is right, and more often than not it is!

Strategically positioned docents direct visitors at each sector threshold, and many more are stationed within its veins. Mini-electric vehicles carry the disabled, elderly, and families with small children who otherwise might be deprived of a grand park adventure. Guided tours are also available. Security, including camera and video surveillance, is tight everywhere, and guards roam every visitor path at close time intervals to keep visitors out of mischief and mishap, and, of course, to protect park residents.

Gorilla Mountain

In our park's northwest corner, the large herbivore track circumscribes a good part of "Gorilla Mountain" before turning south. It is home to our "great apes."* A spur on the east side of the mountain invites visitors [#1] into a cave. Gorilla Mountain is actually a mock "smoking" volcano, rising a hundred or more feet above the visitor's track, replete with pre-eruption belching and roaring sounds! Visitor's passageways are hidden inside with camouflaged one-way windows so we can see all the action outside. For our edification, educational murals line the walls of the mountain's inner visitor paths. As we will learn on this journey, Zoo Paradise is as much a classroom as a spectator's delight.

*The family Hominidae (hominids), constitute the great apes, including gorillas, orangutans and chimpanzees.

Outside under a thin jungle canopy with descending meadows affording grand views across Zoo Paradise, gorilla families romp and play — the males occasionally brawling in good competitive sport — adults raising their young, everyone ever busy working the food chain strategically supplied and configured by park botanists around the entire mountain. Biologists have also facilitated a breeding program in accordance with the principles of natural selection, and in international coordination with zoo administrators and biologists elsewhere as well as wildlife advocates keeping a close eye on threats to gorilla populations and habitats in the species's native homelands.

Outside, just below the plume of volcanic "smoke" (water vapor?), a breathtaking waterfall — "Paradise Falls" — cascades down the southeastern flank of Gorilla Mountain [#2], forming the headwaters of Big River, our meandering "river track" far below. Exciting animal adventures hidden beneath the river's surface and along its banks await visitors on another leg of our journey.

Elephants and zebras mingle in savannah located in Tarangire National Park in Tanzania, East Africa. Zoo Paradise's grand savannahs will capture the essentials details seen above, and deliver them to our residents.

Journey to the South

Our visitor's track now descends from Gorilla Mountain's western flank and then trails southward, paralleling the resident's large herbivore track. The visitor's track is bordered on the east by an increasingly dense jungle canopy that soon cloaks the floor of Zoo Paradise [#3], concealing numerous "sub-tracks" (or "veins") for other species, also available to visitors. Bands of New and Old World monkeys, some of which are tree dwelling, roam these lower forests of Gorilla Mountain and the nearby Western Jungle.

This is our second leg of the visitor track, but this time we are immediately adjacent to the large herbivore track. We are now literally *vis-à-vis* the large animals moving upon it, some of whom are towering above us in height! But, as with the large apes, we are separated from them and out of reach in our own track. Here, we can now see small herds of lumbering elephants, giraffes, zebras and other ungulates, each moving along the same track as complementary foragers. Our own track's close proximity enables us to hear their many fascinating sounds as they make them, and their unique odors fill our nostrils. The experience is exhilarating, for not even but rarely in the wild can humans venture so close in safety!

Just ahead, we will enter the Western Savannah of Zoo Paradise.* This is a large, dry, grass biome where our diverse herds can rest, dust themselves in rolling areas, visit a small lake for drinking and mud baths, camp out, frolic, and nibble at special forages suited to their species that are planted and/or set out by park staff. Because the Western Savannah is only one attractive stop along the large herbivore track for the animals, the motivation to stay put permanently is weak. Curiosity and other needs will provide the necessary impetus to keep these large animal residents moving forward through Zoo Paradise.

Western Savannah

As we enter the savannah [#4], our own track bifurcates and one leg turns to the west above the resident's track (which has widened to form the savannah), the other traverses to the east and then southward. Going to the west, we ascend an immense bridge that spans high above the entire plain, giving visitors a broad and detailed bird's-eye view of resident activities below. There we may see families of elephants, rhinoceros, antelopes, giraffes, zebras, wildebeests, scores of flamingoes on Flamingo Island, ostriches, hares, and more — whatever species our biologists can co-mingle as complementary prey-animal feeders. From above, visitors can take in the entire panoply of exotic sounds, smells, bizarre land formations (including termite mounds), and colors. There are over 1,100 mammal species alone in Africa, and Zoo Paradise administrators have given us an important representation of many, both large and small.

Strategically positioned park docents on the Western Observation Platform [#5] remind visitors to lower their voices — we are there to observe not interact. Alternatively, we are told, we can return to the lower leg of the track on the east side where discussion is encouraged with park rangers sequestered within unique observation rooms to give talks about the animals living just outside in the savannah. Here, the Western Savannah affords visitors additional unprecedented views of residents and their activities. A labyrinth of subterranean passageways criss-cross the plain with numerous windows at the water hole, rolling areas, and campsites.

There's more than meets the eye at first to see on this leg of the journey. On the opposite side of the savanna, to the east, are more excursions. One visitor track heads northerly along Falls Creek [#6] into the homeland of the arboreal monkeys we skirted earlier below Gorilla Mountain. Moving southeasterly, we will reach the Western Jungle [#7], inhabited by large predator cats who, with stealth, will "work the fence line" of the resident's track — under our path! — just "in case" there's easy prey! The smell of "wild prey" is more than these apex predators can stand. Lions live and scout their territory in

*Savannah or savanna: a tropical or subtropical grassland (as of eastern Africa or northern South America) containing scattered trees and drought-resistant undergrowth.

the immediate jungle ahead, and their powerful roars have already been heard more than once across the Western Savannah, even reaching residents atop Gorilla Mountain. Such vocalizations create a natural prey-predator tension in the psyche of our herbivore community, whose vitality is strengthened by it. We'll visit them later on in one of the veins of Zoo Paradise that penetrate the Western African Jungle from the south.

Some of our residents will hold ground and camp in this savannah for the night, for in the next passage they must move past dense jungle canopy and the nearby feline predators, as well as two river crossings where nearby hippos and alligators may challenge their intrusions. Eventually they will reach the distant Eastern Savannah — the park's most easterly boundary — where they will find new forage and fresh water. Let's get going now as the towering bridge and lower visitor tracks have reunited at the jungle's edge [#8], beckoning visitors and residents alike to pass through this exciting, and, at times, eerie traverse across the southern sector of Zoo Paradise.

Rain Forest

At the southeasterly end of the Western Savannah, the visitor's track divides once more, one paralleling the large animal track for those wishing to follow the various herds in their easterly migration to the Eastern Savannah; the other moving northward into the park's Rain Forest [#9]. Here, visitors are treated to a skillfully constructed, discrete labyrinth of resident mini-tracks, swamps, caves, and lairs. Its ambient flora are perpetually soaked by constant misting and torrential rains evoked by strategically positioned micro-irrigation technology. These provide homes to furtive life in the understory and dense canopy of trees: goliath tarantulas, a myriad of amphibians including the endangered tree frog, vampire bats, the Scarlet Macaw and other exotic birds, the black caiman, anacondas, and the elusive jaguar. Snakes, too, are present, including the evasive, but at times highly aggressive when threatened, and venomous Black Mamba, all dwelling on their own tracks, with unique enclosures that abut visitor tracks. This unique microcosm of the world's greatest biodiversity will require one week alone to fathom, let alone see all of its constituents!

Here, as in the Western Jungle to the north with which it converges, biologists identify which live prey are appropriate for which predator, such as the carnivorous cats to hunt and, for the most part, derive all their nutritional needs. Hunting times are posted, and, when diurnal, visitors are welcome to observe the hunts in their entirety. Everywhere, educational dioramas pepper the visitor's tracks, explaining the interesting complexities of each species — including their feeding behaviors — inhabiting each sector of Zoo Paradise. As in the Western Savannah, the unique construction of the visitor's tracks and camouflaged observation posts within the jungle bring to life the sights, smells, and

Black mamba in defensive posture.

sounds of its rain forest residents.

Visitors wishing for a unique culinary divertissement may enjoy the sylvan Rain Forest Café [#10], an unimaginable repasting experience for any zoological garden. Built upon stilts with walls of glass, and with a direct view to wilderness vitality, the visitor truly feels a profound sense of oneness with the spirit of Zoo Paradise.

Back on the large herbivore track, residents migrate northeasterly in distinct herds composed of family units, whose members move single-file according to relative dominance. On their northern flank, the herds remain vigilant as the big cats, ever curious, and ready to strike youthful family members of any of the large herbivores, patrol the entire eastern and southern edges of their jungle territory — all along Rain Forest Creek, where they may lap water before its confluence with Big River. There alligators patrol the shores, and our herd must again remain vigilant of these additional apex predators.

On the southern flank of the large herbivore track, the jungle soon gives way to the first hints of alpine tundra and the rising Southern Alps — the highest reach of the park,

rivaling Disneyland's Matterhorn, and home to the mountain goat. With its breathtaking views, the Alps are truly one of the grand adventures awaiting visitors. We will ascend its highest peaks by electric train (or tram) later in our tour when we visit the resident goat families high up in alps.

Returning to the large herbivore track, we and the herds lumber along northeasterly towards Big River, the ground rumbling below the weight of elephant footsteps. For visitors on their adjacent track, the elephants, giraffes, rhinoceri and others cast an extraordinary contrast with the alps in the background — not unlike Mount Kilimanjaro rising above the savannah (*above*, and *pages 1-2*). There is little doubt shutter-bugs, camcorders, and similar electronic species are also busy on this leg of the journey!

Big River

Visitors and residents alike now trek eastward, and approach Big River due north of the alps. This will be the first of several river crossings by our residents. Visitors may continue in parallel manner with the residents, or divert up (north) or downstream (south) along the river [#11] or continue forward onto the park's Central Observation Platform [#12]. Going north or south visitors enjoy the "Big River Odyssey" — arguably the park's most exciting visitor adventure. Here the visitor's track stretches the length of central Big River. Living beneath the track both within and along the banks of the river are some of Zoo Paradise's most exciting residents: alligators and hippos. Both present challenges to our terrestrial herbivores — elephants, giraffes, zebras, and other "prey" species — who must now make their first river crossing in their journey to foraging grounds in the Eastern Savannah. Alligators are known predators, and hippos are also feared for their territorial aggressiveness against other species. Zoo Paradise biologists have configured a way to release prey animals for feeding the gators, thereby "sparing" our residents on the large herbivore track as they ford the river ("first crossing"). At the same time, nearby hippos "pressure" the residents to get across and continue down their track to the "second crossing" of Big River. Along the way, both residents and visitors pass below a unique bridge over which the barely audible electric train passes on its way up to the Southern Alps — the "grand finale" of our tour, which is coming up soon. At the second crossing, there are shallow, but noisy, rapids which must be traversed by the residents. This is a transition zone leading into the Great Outback, which they must circumscribe before reaching the Eastern Savannah. Let's go there now!

Great Outback

The Great Outback features a colorful spectrum of forest, plant, barren landscapes, and animal species endemic to the "down under" continent of Australia and nearby island country of New Zealand. Koalas inhabit Zoo Paradise's pungent Eucalyptus Forest. Goannas — monitor lizards — roam the entire Outback as they are adapted to a range of environments. Kiwis, a threatened species of flightless bird from New Zealand, range on the eponymous Kiwi Island, a sister island to Flamingo Island in the Western Savannah, safe from bands of dingoes roaming the Outback savannah and forest microcosms. Kangaroos, Tasmanian Devils, and other species also pepper this easternmost expanse of Zoo Paradise.

Along this stretch of the large herbivore track, visitors have several options. One [#13], to continue coursing alongside the large herbivore track, taking excursions into the eastern Outback savannah to see interesting rock formations, kangaroo and wallaby pods, Kiwi Island, and also — from within subterranean observation galleries — observe microcosms filled with strange and fascinating creatures: reptiles, amphibians, spiders, and insects in simulated natural habitats and that are native species to the Australian continent.

Alternatively, visitors can head "inland" to see the Koalas in the nearby Eucalyptus Forest [#14]. From there, they can continue on to the Eastern Savannah, where they can also ford a bridge leading to Turtle Island.

Eastern Savannah

At last residents and visitors have reached the large herbivore Eastern Savannah.

A kangaroo pod on the move at sunrise in the Great Outback.

Here, residents, arriving in distinct herd units delineated by RD, drink their fill at Big Lake, and then spread out across the plain. Some family groups will feed and then overnight here to sleep, while others will rest and then continue on during the night, feeding along the way until they seek repose either on track or come full circle at the Western Savannah. Visitors can circumscribe the plain to the west, and visit turtle island where various species of turtles reside, (and also observe the large herbivores take water and bathe); or continue north and ascend the overhead bridge to peer down upon the residents and the vast plain from the observation deck as they may have at the Western Savannah [#15].

Bear Mountain

Bear Mountain provides visitors with a North American wilderness experience. This unique biome of Zoo Paradise represents another great challenge for park biologists, who must be selective and able to integrate a diversity of wildlife. Visitors may enter anyone of several veins and observation posts trickling through the wilderness area, around which wild horses, antelope, and bison move in small herds on a winding track, at times paralleling the large herbivore track, and at other times in near shot of stealthful mountain lions. Ancient ancestors of the horse, bison, lion and elephant once mingled in North America 8-10,000 years ago, many becoming extinct during the late Pleistocene Epoch. Interestingly, Zoo Paradise has brought back together family lineages who did survive elsewhere on the planet.

Various North American wildlife inhabit Bear Mountain, including wolves, moose, eagles, deer, and bears. A popular visitor's vein leads high up Bear Mountain, home to the park's family of bears [#16]. Here visitors are treated to close-up views from camouflaged observation dens within the mountain of one of the most dynamic simulations of wilderness living by a species in captivity.

Spring-fed Bear Lake [#17] is the fountainhead of Bear Creek, flowing down into Big Lake.* Up and down the banks and here and there mid-stream along Bear Creek, bears catch fat-rich salmon ascending the river and its rapids upstream from the lake. The "daily catch" has become a park favorite of visitors too! In the nearby forests, bears also scour the edges of their tracks for vegetation selected by park biologists and botanists. In some instances, carrion originating here and from other sectors of Zoo Paradise is delivered to the bear tracks in the spring by staff to round out their diet.

*Water in Big Lake is filtered and returned by pumps to both Bear Lake and Gorilla Mountain.

Mountain lions also inhabit this sector of Zoo Paradise, and park biologists counterpose them with deer, elk, and moose to exert the predation force. At regular intervals, these prey-predator residents are brought together to facilitate feline hunts, insuring species vitality, population control, and the forces of natural selection. Also in the forests are owls and other large birds-of-prey, which feed upon ground squirrels, rabbits, snakes, and other suitable prey animals slithering and scurrying about in the mountain forest understory. It should not go without mentioning that the visitor's ascent of Bear Mountain also affords dramatic views westward across Zoo Paradise.

Final leg of the tour

Back on the large herbivore track in the Eastern Savannah, many of our family herds have watered, foraged, and, as has been the case since the Western Savannah, are ready to move on in well-defined formations based on species and pecking order. Moving past Bear Mountain, they soon reach Zoo Paradise's "Grand Entrance." As our large herbivores continue westward to gorilla mountain and points beyond, we will take leave of absence of this visitor's track and move directly south to the Southern Alps. The track leading to and from the alps is arguably the most awesome experience in Zoo Paradise. To reach the alps we must first stop at the park's Central Observation Platform [#12], another masterpiece of our park's architects and engineers. The platform rises above the surrounding forest canopies and savannahs giving visitors a 360 degree view of Zoo Paradise's diverse and fascinating landscapes. It also serves as an internal staging and information center, from which informed visitors can choose which park sector they wish to see first. Many visitors will loop back to the platform as their preferred staging area, while others will avail themselves to other strategies. But we will continue south to the alps, in fact, the southern end of the platform is the boarding station for the electric train (or tram) that will take us to the alp's summit — the highest elevation in all of Zoo Paradise!

Visitors ride the airway gondola to the pinnacle of the Southern Alps. Below, an electric train ferries visitors along a winding path to the same summit, and Zoo Paradise's highest observation deck, affording dramatic views of the entire park.

Southern Alps Adventure

From the south port of the Central Observation Platform, visitors board either the park's sleek and surprisingly noiseless electric train for the gradual ascent of the Southern Alps, or the more direct ascent via the airway tram. Views immediately below along the way include the hippo lagoon, Big River, and the Large Herbivore and visitor tracks — all of which we visited earlier. As the train/tram ascends higher up the north face of the alps, spectacular panoramic views of the entire park unfold. The train slowly winds its way upward and between the peaks of the alps. Along the way, the first of many mountain goats appear, foraging and negotiating the steep inclines as few species can. Park engineers have skillfully crafted snow and icescapes here and there on the slopes of the alps, frequented often and instinctively so by the residents whose fur coats offer a specialized adaptation to sustain their homeostasis and vitality.

Near the summit of the alps, the train reaches the highest observation platform in Zoo Paradise, where visitors may disembark to take in the spectacular views of the entire park and vistas far beyond. Here, too, park engineers have crafted snow drifts and caches, and hidden fans simulating mountain winds and sounds to give visitors a sense of the residents' high altitude climate. Visitors are warmed by hot cocoas, coffee, and teas from the only vendor on the platform. From this platform, visitors may return to the Central Observation Platform via the train/tram, or enter a passage that leads inside the mountain to a dramatic spiral pathway that gently descends to the bottom, where it intersects the visitors track that parallels the Large Herbivore track. A waterfall lies at the center of the spiral pathway inside the mountain here, blossoming into the fresh water lagoon our large herbivores may take water from — if nearby hippos do not make much a fuss! Visitors also take an exciting stroll behind the falls to connect to their track that skirts the edge of the lagoon. Within the mountain, open panoramic view windows afford light and fresh air, while selectively positioned lights amplify the beauty of the central waterfall which casts a pleasant mist to cool the passage during the hottest summer months.

§

Summary

The preceding tour is simply a conceptual template for action of which I imagine many possible variations. Location, climate, availability of land and resources, which residents and how many will live there, and the vision and dedication of zoo administrators, engineers, planners, and scientists, will converge as determinants to press out each possibility. For me, and many horse owners, the triumphs of Paddock Paradise that have inured to the benefit and vitality of horses otherwise "trapped" in oppressive and inhumane living conditions — sad parodies of what nature intended — followed from the same challenges that the progenitors of Zoo Paradise will also face and have to overcome. But the path has been laid.

CHAPTER SIX
Paradise Pragmatics

No unprecedented conceptual model of wildlife habitat, particularly habitat artificially positioned at the center of civilization, could be seriously considered if there is no attention given to pragmatism. Certainly this was the case with Paddock Paradise, when initially wave after wave of resistance to the idea, drowning as it was in a stream of every imaginable excuse, came from every stronghold of conventional horse keeping practices, "Such a proposal will not work for horses." Much of this discordance was embedded in bogus ideas about the very biology of the horse. It seemed that too many horse owners were influenced heavily by what they saw in Hollywood westerns, at race tracks, and in local stall barns. The mere suggestion of creating habitats for their horses based on free-roaming horses living in the wild was simply too much of a clash with their own experiences and with what their experts were telling them! After emerging from my first foray into wild horse country in 1982, I even recall one of my clients recoiling in terror as I announced with great delight that I would forthwith be conducting "wild horse trims" on her horse. Her response, "I don't want anything 'wild' on my horse," made me nearly drop my tools on the ground in shock. The term "natural trim", used widely and respectfully across the horse world today, was born of that negative experience over 37 years ago. As I write these words, I'm wondering now if Zoo Paradise, with thousands of species involved, won't conjure up tidal waves of resistance too!

What follows are some of the practical issues that we have been confronted with in Paddock Paradise. Zoo Paradise will have them too, but on a larger scale. Most "problems" are soluble when solutions are given a wide berth of experimentation. In fact, following the Hediger Rule of returning to the wild to see what the animals do themselves as a consequence of natural selection is key. In fact, this is what I did at every step of the way at the AANHCP Field Headquarters — asking myself, what did the wild ones do? And what can we do to bridge the gaps created by domestication? At that point, the "devil is in the details" of experimentation, and creative minds are very welcome too! Let me give an example that required much "trial and error" in how we feed horses "naturally" based on the "lessons from the wild" — and I'm fairly sure what we arrived at will find its way into Zoo Paradise, as well.

The horse's relatively small stomach provides a vital clue about how we should feed him (what we feed him is another issue!). In the wild, equines are adapted to nibbling a range of things, never much quantity of anything in one place, and pretty much on the move constantly as forage is scarce. Dr. Ric Redden, an equine veterinarian and surgeon who conducted a study of 1,800 wild horses in the U.S. Great Basin, would write after visiting their rangelands, "There is more grass growing on the paper I am writing this report on than can be found on 100 acres of their natural habitat." What this means is that horses naturally eat small amounts at a time and, therefore, must do a lot of moving to get to where there is forage to consume. So, the small stomach — followed by a long intestinal tract — is the perfect adaptation to process food into the lower intestines to "wring out" as much nutrition as possible. Yet, it is commonplace in domestication to stuff horses with feed in just one or two "set meals." No wonder that colic, the number one horse killer, is epidemic across the horse world. Further, because the stomach remains empty for long stretches at a time, digestive acid (hydrochloric acid) leads to ulcers that also favor colonies of harmful acid loving bacteria, resulting in uncomfortable horses. Antacids aren't going to work, but, fortunately, Paddock Paradise solves the problem by feeding in a manner their closely simulates what happens in the wild.

To get in step with natural equine feeding behaviors, we set out a mixture of different hays (their principal forage) into nets suspended from poles, one net per horse thereby forming a "feed station," as we called it, and positioning a number of feed stations along their main track. The nets preclude the horse from gorging, but do allow small amounts to the "plucked" from the net, which simulates the prehensile manner in which they pluck dry bunch grasses and other flora in the wild with their lips and teeth. Presto — problem solved! Unfortunately, it took us over a year to figure out all the "details" to make it work. We experimented with as many ways to pack the hay, as we did in making the poles and hanging hardware work, and transporting the hay to the feed stations. Not to forget trying to figure out where to put those stations too! In the end, the effort and frustration was worth it, because it is reflected in the extraordinary vitality of our horses who were admired by all our visitors.

What follows are some of the issues that we faced and solved in the ongoing evolution of our Paddock Paradise, and that will surely arise in any Zoo Paradise. Most are derived from the behavior chart at the front of Chapter 5, which will apply to all species in some measure. My philosophy in whatever we do with the horse in the realm of NHC is to keep it as simple, efficient, and natural (i.e., humane) as possible — and hopefully this will work for the animals of Zoo Paradise as well. And in so doing, we can be assured the outcome will be both welcoming and inspiring to the visitor, at the same time delivering vitality to the residents.

Copraphragy and Dung Management

In 2012, I spoke before government conservation agents of Washington State about the potential benefits of incorporating Paddock Paradise in ecologically sound land management practices. One concern was that horses and other livestock were a constant threat to fragile riparian systems (e.g., springs, streams, and rivers) in the Pacific Northwest. By entering such a sensitive waterway, and entire ecology could be wiped out from trampling and waste contamination, which may also include the many drugs and chemical agents horse and other livestock owners treat their animals with. One of the senior managers had discovered my book *Paddock Paradise*, put a track together for her personal horses, and immediately saw its implications on a broader scale. The invitation to speak followed. By using the Paddock Paradise tracking system, animals can be kept away from sensitive areas in part or entirely.

Another area of concern by the Washington land agents centered around composting. I suggested that dung be removed from the tracks and processed in conjunction with the State's current programs to compost animal and other biodegradable farm wastes. Dung can also be spread over pastures adjacent to the track, and some left within the track as territorial markers (e.g., "stud piles" in wild horse country), and — prior to biodegradation — it serves as a nutrient source for the animals themselves, as the species is coprophagous at an early age. Although controversial and the mechanisms are yet to be elucidated, advocates like myself believe that there is evidence that coprophagy is intrinsic in some measure to sustaining vital microbial balances in the digestive tract. The horses at the AANHCP Field Headquarters were never given parasiticides, nor were they infested. Neither are wild horses of the U.S. Great Basin.

How much dung is acceptable in Zoo Paradise? Part of the answer lies in how much (quantity) exists within the total living/tracking space occupied by the species living in the wild. Biologists who have studied those environments would be the right persons to do the math. By gathering data for what is known in domestication, that is, by studying "control groups" in a controlled environment, then doing a head count in the wild in a given home range and attributing weight values accordingly, and finally dividing that quantity by the area occupied, a ratio of "dung-weight/acre" can be calculated. If the ratio derived for the Zoo Paradise tracks exceeds that calculated for native home ranges, then dung must be extracted. If less, it can stay. By extrapolation, animal-units could also be calculated per acre, providing a way for biologists to determine how many animals can occupy a given Zoo Paradise track in a biodynamically balanced environment, thereby avoiding "overpopulation." This data, in turn, would prove useful in orchestrating breeding programs within Zoo Paradise.

During my last visit to the San Diego Zoo at Balboa Park, I noticed that dung "movement" by means of heavy equipment was a fairly steady affair as residents had no choice but to create an abundance of body wastes in their close confinement environments. Of course, it is possible that any presence of dung would be construed as "unpleasant" for gawking visitors, and so removal was imperative no matter what the quantity. Under the circumstances, therefore, normal biodegradation that we see in the wild (and in the AANHCP Paddock paradise) might be problematic. As a solution, Zoo Paradise would retain "wanted" dung within the tracking system, making it available for natural interspecies coprophagy (e.g., the dung/scarab beetle — a single dung beetle can bury dung that is 250 times heavier than itself in one night.), soil and waterway enrichment, and fertilizer for internal and external track flora. Where natural or artificial rain is possible, soaking the ground would expedite absorption of wastes — assuming riparian systems are not going to be threatened in a given biosphere of Zoo Paradise. Excess waste management would follow the Washington State model for extraction, composting and redistribution. In this way, Zoo Paradise would prosper from appropriate levels of biodegradable waste as do the natural environments from which the animals were derived in the wild.

Prevention of disease, injuries and lameness

There are several sides to this discussion. First, according to NHC science, disease is a consequence of compromised vitality. For example, heavy smokers tend to die from cancer, heavy drinkers from cirrhosis of the liver, coal miners from "black lung", and people who do not exercise and eat little but junk food tend to die from heart disease or complications of diabetes. Vitality has its limits. Animals living in zoos today have parallel health risks stemming from close confinement (lack of exercise and socialization), questionable diets, boredom and depression, and neurotic behaviors that can be dangerous to themselves and fellow "inmates."

In contrast to disease, there is biomechanical breakdown, that is, "lameness" due to body trauma. In the wild, most serious trauma debilitation results from predation and male rivalry for females. The outcomes can be pretty serious, including death, but that's part of the cycle of life in the wild in keeping with natural selection. That will be less of an issue in Zoo Paradise, although, as I mentioned in the previous chapter, I believe controlled predation should be part of life "on track" in some measure. But, for the most part, Zoo Paradise should be designed to facilitate "close encounters" — threats that cannot come to deadly fruition. Minor traumatic injuries are actually very common in the wild, and certainly that was the case among our horses at the AANHCP Field Headquarters. Kicking, biting, charging, pinning the ears, etc., are as common as the setting sun. But most of these displays are just that — harmless threats to remind another of their position in the ranks of the social order. Some of this is even amusing to the human eye and awareness. For example, our buckskin Chance is definitely one muscular, physically fit, and athletic chum. But his demeanor is that of a beta. In fact, until we closed the headquarters, he was very near the bottom of his family band's pecking order. He did constantly irritate our monarch alpha, Apollo, who very reliably gave Chance a pounding for it. Chance just stood there often to take his beating. But nature selects for this, and so we simply observed but did not interfere. There is also male bonding, in which the dominant member will bite the hide of another whom he is actually quite found of. This is also the plight of Chance, who takes it all. At times, Apollo really escalates because Chance will not let up bothering him, and Chance will run to keep out of reach. This is usually no more than 10 to 15 feet, as Apollo has made his point, and Chance is too beta to move any further away from his family. If RD is a centrifugal force in the natural world of socialization, then the herd/family instinct is an equally powerful centripetal force to keep family members intact within their family's social network I should add that truly serious fighting among horses is the providence of the male domain. Females may squabble and kick at each other — or, and this is hard to believe — pound away with both hind hooves at once on a male suitor whom they actually favor! "Love taps" would be the understatement of the year, nevertheless, both parties are selected for this type of behavior, and, in the next moment they may be breeding, mutually grooming, or eating quietly together. This was what I observed in the wild, and this is what we facilitated in Paddock Paradise. RD unquestionably serves vitality.

Foot care

Foot care is my area of professional expertise, and because foot problems plague countless horses and other hoofed animals in domestication, and commensurately captive wild animals in zoos, I'll offer some of my insights on the subject.[1] There is a saying in my profession, "If the foot goes, so goes the animal." Indeed, euthanasia is alarmingly epidemic in the horse-using community because the foot is so misunderstood and mistreated. Which is to say it is "blamed" (so to speak) for problems that, in fact, originate elsewhere in the horse's body. Nature has configured the hoof to express itself symptomatically with aberrant growth patterns and pain that can be traced very specifically to disease and biomechanical dysfunction matrixed above the hoof line. When these relationships are not understood, mismanaged hoof care typically ensues, which only exacerbates matters, drawing the animals into a vicious cycle of compromised vitality and misery cited previously by Walt Taylor. Once more, this takes us right back to the Hagen-

[1]See my published advanced texts on natural hoof care: *The Natural Trim: Basic Guidelines: Trim Mechanics, Biodynamics, and Healing Forces in Paddock Paradise -- Working with Nature to Create the Perfect Hoof* (2019) and *The Natural Trim: Advanced Guidelines: Healing Pathology in the 4th Dimension* (2019).

beck-Hediger axis — pathology will follow from unnatural habitats and lifestyles — and, I will add, foot care very specifically.

The very premise of Zoo Paradise is rooted in the presumption of vitality, meaning we are principally concerned with *preventive care* that precludes disease, lameness, psychological distress, and, therefore, lives of misery. And not to diminish the role of preventive care in the treatment of pathology, the very instruments of preventive care are in their own right often enough to successfully treat disease, injuries and lameness.

The many hoofed residents of Zoo Paradise sooner or later will need their feet tended to, but we hope minimally so because of their naturalized lifestyles. At the AANHCP Field Headquarters, horses are given the "natural trim" modeled after the wild, free-roaming horse of the U.S. Great Basin. The principles underlying that trim are actually universal to all hoofed animals, including those of Zoo Paradise. While trim mechanics — entailing use of tools/equipment, horse handling skills (RD), body positioning, knowledge of major structures of foot/hoof and their physiology, pathophysiology, and simulation of natural wear patterns — are very technical and beyond the scope of this book, a discussion of the principles guiding the trim — based on the laws of nature — is pertinent. In this discussion, I will reference the horse, assuming that biologists and hoof care practitioners of Zoo Paradise will interpolate the nuances of other species in their interpretations.

At the core of the natural trim is the very meaning of the word *natural.* There is some warranted confusion here — given the standard dictionary definition of the word quoted at right — whether a trim method can be defined as natural when human "intervention" is involved at all in the process. Arguably, the term natural has been so wantonly savaged through commercial exploitation and gimmickry that the answer calls for an immediate and resounding "no." Such denigration aside, however, the horse's foot has proven to be more than tolerant of us in the matter of trimming — inviting actually — when we rise to the laws of nature and apply certain common sense *principles* based upon them in our work. When we do this, bogus and exploitative dimensions to the word *natural* quickly fall by the wayside, while genuine meaning stands firmly in their place. Such is the reality of the *natural trim* when anchored firmly to these principles, as is the whole of NHC based on the animal's natural state.

natural - existing in nature; in accordance with the principles of nature; as formed by nature without human intervention; wild condition.

When we speak in terms of, or act upon, nature's principles for guiding the natural trim, it is implicit that the adaptation of *Equus ferus caballus* is a constant undercurrent either giving, or taking away, impetus to anything done to the hoof. This ancient force, the culmination of 55 million years of evolutionary descent, cannot be ignored; to the contrary, it must be understood, integrated, and cultured through the broad holistic spec-

trum of NHC practices. The natural trim, for certain, even with its own spectra of complex, interventional mechanics, cannot stand alone to bring the domesticated hoof into
alignment and harmony with the underlying forces of nature. NHC practitioners understand that to successfully execute the trim in accordance with nature's guiding principles
within the holistic fold, there must be ethical adherence to two timeless tenets derived
from the 5th century BCE Hippocratic Oath and observed by all responsible health care
practitioners and humanitarians ever since:

> *Primum non nocere* — First, do no harm.
> *vis medicatrix naturae* — Respect the healing powers of nature.

These are truly inspiring words to abide by, and my opinion is that the horse world, and
hoof care providers of all disciplines in particular, could do much to get in step with
them! Nature's guiding principles for the trim flow readily from these two admonitions.

When I first wrote the natural trim guidelines, I included what I refer to as the
"Four Guiding Principles of the Natural Trim". These are based entirely on the wild
horse model, and, therefore, connect us directly to nature's principles and the powerful
forces of adaptation that created the horse's foot through the evolutionary descent of
Equus ferus caballus through natural selection. The first three principles cross-link to the
first Hippocratic admonition to do no harm; the fourth principle "indirectly" connects
us to the second admonition to "respect the healing powers of nature". I would not think
of trimming the horse's foot without these Guiding Principles in mind at every moment.
They have brought me peace of mind as a NHC practitioner over the past 40 years, and
certainty that my efforts are always in the best interest of the horse:

The Four Guiding Principles of the Natural Trim

1. Leave that which naturally should be there. Refers to the protection and preserva-
tion by the trimmer of the integrity of the basic anatomical parts of the hoof, such as the
frog, bars, sole, and hoof wall. Principle #1 speaks to the "do no harm" clause since
these structures are routinely removed excessively — and not infrequently — altogether
surgically by inappropriate farrier, veterinary, and "generic" barefoot trim methods. I
view such excesses as inhumane, entirely unnecessary, and contraindicated by NHC principles and methodology governed by the wild horse model.

2. Remove only that which is naturally worn away in the wild. This means that
when the hoof (i.e., epidermis or capsule) is reduced by the trimmer, only that which
would be worn away in the horse's wild state is taken. Principle #2 also implies that
which is being removed should be trimmed away because it is excess growth. Similar to
violations of Principle #1, the do no harm clause is invoked when excessive capsule is

removed.

3. Allow to grow that which should be there naturally but isn't due to human med-dling. Instructs the trimmer to use restraint when faced with hooves that have been over-trimmed in some part (such as a heel-buttress), and, particularly, to refrain from remov-ing epidermis from the opposing structure (e.g., the opposite heel-buttress) so as to es-tablish an ersatz "balance" that only worsens matters for the horse. This also applies to misguided efforts to force one hoof (e.g., the left front) to look like the other (the right front), for example, by over-thinning part of a hoof wall. Finally, Principle #3 admon-ishes the trimmer to not compensate the over-trimmed hoof by using horseshoes, wedg-ing technology, and acrylics to "give it a better angle". As always, the trimmer is to give the hoof time to heal, grow and renew its own structure.   In fact, the hoof possesses this inherent self-healing capability.

4. Ignore all pathology. Warns the trimmer not to focus on pathology (if present) or violations of the three previous principles, but, instead, to look intuitively to 4th-dimensional changes (healing changes over time — "respect the healing powers of na-ture") and faithfully adhere to NHC principles and practices. Although this principle ap-pears to be an oxymoron, in practice it is true when the proven practices of NHC are im-plemented. Pathology invariably takes care of itself when we do healthful things. Princi-ple #4 also applies to the risks of "dirty window syndrome", that is, obsession with mi-nutia, perfection, and pathology — a proven corridor to invasive, harmful trimming and violations of Principle #2. It is easier to see and understand nature's 4-D healing forces through the lens of vitality, than through disease, and one is then less like to fall victim to "fixing" problems rather than focusing on emerging health based on holistic care.

Natural Trim Defined

Technically, the natural trim is concerned with and defined as the humane transpos-ing or "mimicking" of natural *wear patterns* documented in wild horse feet (or any hoofed animal for our purposes in Zoo Paradise) onto the hooves of domesticated horses. When these wear patterns are diligently and repeatedly applied to the hoof at roughly 4-6 week time intervals, the natural trim (governed by the Four Guiding Princi-ples) triggers a cascade of integrated biodynamic (i.e., living) forces that produce and re-inforce natural growth patterns that result in naturally shaped hooves. This melding of forces is sometimes described as a reinforcing "cycle of form and function." This cycle (*Overleaf*), in reality, defines the specific role and limits of the natural trim. And active within its penumbra are the collateral influences of each horse's unique temperamental character and physical conformation, the environment, and, never to be underestimated or ignored, the impact of human meddling. Briefly, let's follow the cyclical force field

Overleaf — cycle of form and function in natu-ral hoof care.

Relationship of the natural trim to the biodynamic cycle of form and function

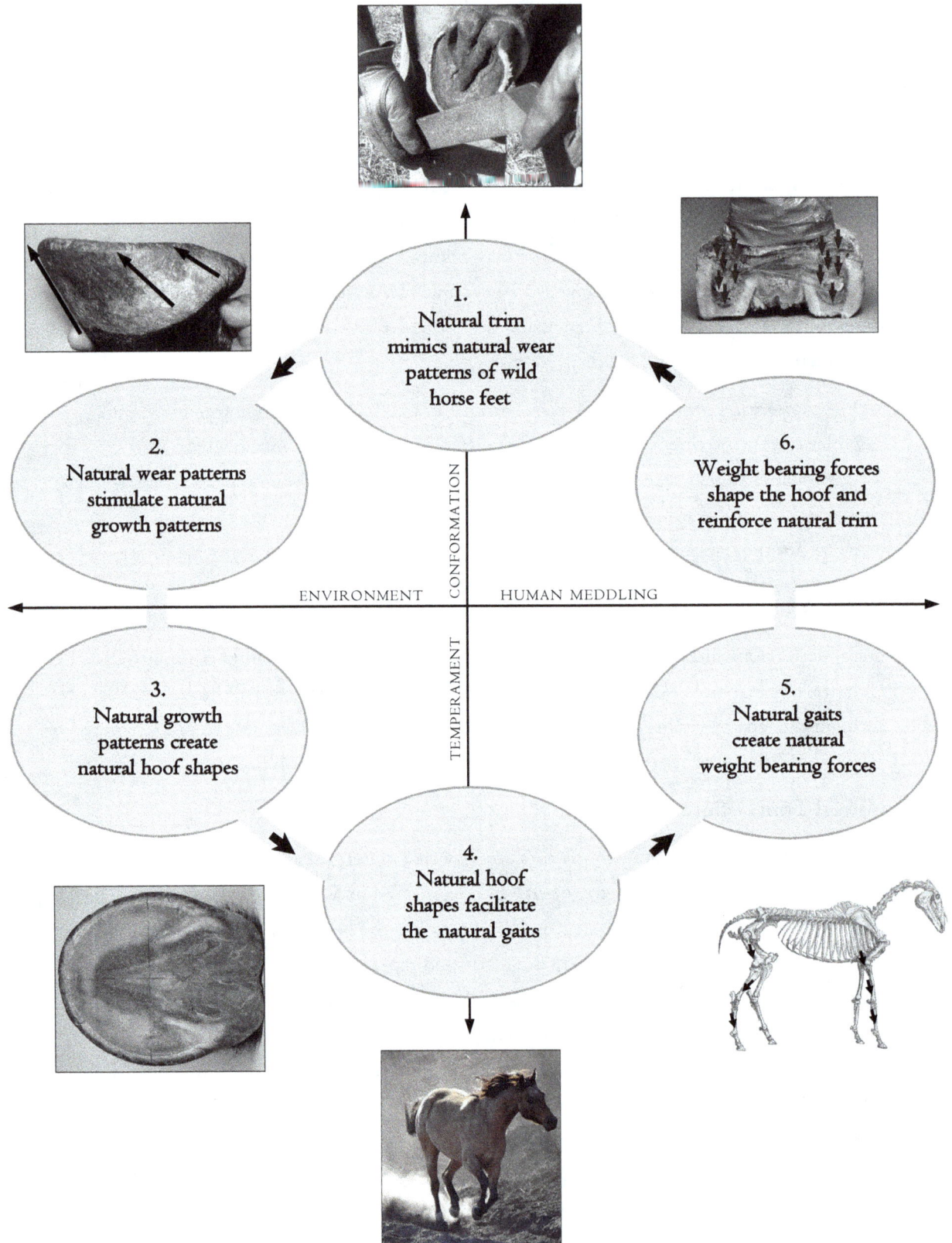

1.
Natural trim mimics natural wear patterns of wild horse feet

2.
Natural wear patterns stimulate natural growth patterns

6.
Weight bearing forces shape the hoof and reinforce natural trim

CONFORMATION

ENVIRONMENT   HUMAN MEDDLING

TEMPERAMENT

3.
Natural growth patterns create natural hoof shapes

5.
Natural gaits create natural weight bearing forces

4.
Natural hoof shapes facilitate the natural gaits

diagrammatically laid out in the *overleaf* that follows from the natural trim:

I. Natural trim mimics natural wear patterns of wild horse feet.

The cycle begins as the NHC practitioner trims the hoof by mimicking the *natural wear patterns* seen in the wild. This is done regardless of the damage done to the foot due to shoeing, unnatural trimming methods, and lifestyle complications. The Four Guiding Principles govern how this is achieved without causing harm while respecting and incorporating the individual horse's unique conformation and other attributes that will always influence future hoof growth (size, shape and proportion). This step ends the trimmer's role at the hoof; other NHC holistic practices are then implemented.

2. Natural wear patterns stimulate natural growth patterns.

Immediately following the trim, the foot's sensitive (innervated) and vascular dermal structures responsible for creating the capsule (the foot's epidermal armor) respond by producing growth patterns that correspond to the natural wear patterns. This characteristic growth response seems to be driven genetically by the powerful underlying adaptive force. New growth will reach ground level in approximately 9 months, that is, one *hoof growth cycle* (*hgc*) or the time it takes for the foot to completely reproduce itself.

3. Natural growth patterns create natural hoof shapes.

With each subsequent trim session, the generated growth patterns continue to position mass in the direction of the underlying adaptive form, in effect, posturing the capsule for optimal locomotive function. To be clear, the foot is *not* adapting to the environment, but is overcoming the pernicious effects of misguided human meddling. The result is a hoof that, under the influence of NHC holistic interventions, becomes increasingly more naturally shaped over time with each trim — called 4th dimensional (4D) changes in hoof mass. I view these efforts as a quest of sorts to tip the scales of "holistic" and antagonistic "anti-holistic" forces in favor of the naturally shaped hoof.

4. Natural shapes facilitate the natural gaits.

The initial growth pattern response to the trim, having reached ground level after I *hgc*, now provides a more naturally shaped hoof (size, shape, and proportion) for the horse to move on. The horse can now move more naturally on his feet using his natural gaits. Obviously this is an area of intervention that horse owners can partake in by providing a Paddock Paradise tracking system, and engaging the horse as a natural rider.

5. Natural gaits create natural weight-bearing forces.

The natural gaits now begin to organize and propel weight bearing forces as the horse moves more naturally on his feet. The feet must receive and resist these powerful forces delivered by the natural gaits, and as they do, the hooves are shaped. It is interesting to note that muscle groups, once organized around a less than natural — if not outright pathological — hoof conformation, also begin to transform. This is an interesting phenomenon to observe, particularly in more challenging Paddock Paradises, wherein mass begins to dissipate within the pathological matrix, and simultaneously accrete ("build in") where it should be. It is not uncommon to hear, "My horse looks like an entirely new animal." Conversely, horses removed from these tracking systems undergo a reversal of the NHC form and function cycle.

6. Weight bearing forces shape the hoof and reinforce natural trim.

It almost goes without saying that when natural weight bearing forces have been generated and are at work, a naturally shaped hoof will be the outcome. Certainly this is the case at the AANHCP Field Headquarters, and when the circuitry of the "cycle of vitality" presented here is not broken by ill-conceived or seriously compromised management practices, we should expect the same outcome in Zoo Paradise.

Tracks

The principal idea behind tracks in Zoo Paradise is to provide appropriate space within which individualized paths can be defined by the residents themselves. Tracks for visitors are externalized from resident tracks as explained in Chapter 4 (*Symbiosis*) and characterized in Chapter 5 (*Welcome to Zoo Paradise*). On practical levels, footings in the various pathways must simulate those found in each specie's native rangeland. Equines and other ungulates, for example, will require a range of firm, dry footings to serve their vitality — similar to those described in Paddock Paradise (Chapter 2). In contrast, the amphibious residents living in Big River will require the various features of a healthy, naturally moving waterway, mud and sand embankments, and flora adapted to water. Predator tracks should also intersect — but not conjoin — with prey tracks, once more, to serve vitality.

While I will leave it to biologists serving other species in Zoo Paradise, I would like to offer several solutions for our resident ungulates. This concerns the issue of "mud" that has plagued many a Paddock Paradises in the more rainy climates around the world. I first addressed the problem publicly on the Paddock Paradise Facebook when a horse owner raised the question, "How do I deal with all the mud in my Paddock Paradise, especially where they get their hay." The AANHCP Paddock Paradise was located in a high desert type biome, with gravel everywhere, so we've never shared this person's dilemma. But her query was positioned in relation to a photo of the entrance gate leading into her Paddock Paradise. Outside the gate was her parked car. Immediately, I saw the solution, and answered her call, "How did your car get from the paved road, through a quarter mile of soaked pasture on either side, and out to your Paddock Paradise, without getting stuck in a muddy rut?" The answer, of course, was the narrow gravel road! The next day I visited the road engineer for the City of Lompoc near our own Paddock Paradise to discuss the solution in greater detail.

What is recommended is that one either fill the entire track with road bed — the material that rural county gravel roads are made of, very inexpensive — or, more economical yet, dig a trench within the track and fill it with the road bed. In either case, the ground must be trenched first, then filled, and finally rolled (or trampled down by the horses — or Zoo Paradise residents — themselves). My engineer friend said to do this during the summer so that when the rainy season arrives, the bed will be "set." The trench need not be more than 8 inches deep and just wide enough for horses to travel single file. For equines, 12 to 16 inches wide is sufficient. Zoo Paradise biologists will have to study other resident terrestrial paths in the wild to determine appropriate widths and depths. Most will be surprisingly narrow and the widest not much more than the horse's, even for the massive elephant! Instinctively, residents will forge their own paths within the tracks. Once these are ascertained, a decision can be made either to trench the entire track, or a path within the track. I imagine the large herbivore track will harbor multi-paths, and, therefore, trenching the entire track may be justified.

Another facet of the track concerns the placement of water holes, streams, etc., to facilitate optimal watering behavior. Each species will have its unique needs. Elephants, for example, will need to go into the water to drink and bathe. Nearby should be soil suitable for rolling and "mud baths" — as opposed to rolling and dry dusting sites which should be positioned away from water. Also positioned along and within the track is ample and suitable forage. I've noted that in Paddock Paradise, forage — a range of hays — is fed in hay bags suspended from the ground. This will work for some species in Zoo Paradise, but not others. Grains and minerals can be fed in troughs or mixed in with baled forage. In all cases, the central idea is to deliver vital nutrients in a way that fosters movement, rather than permanent "camping sites."

Last, depending on the location, climate and time of year, some residents will require special temporary housing to protect them from weather elements that are alien to their species and adaptative natural habitat. So as not to adversely impact the "wildness" of Zoo Paradise, which is integral to the vitality of the residents, temporary shelters should be positioned either outside the immediate tracking system but allowing for open access to the tracks, or, if possible, permanent enclosures along the tracks that residents can enter during inclement weather. In either case, their construction would mimic as much as possible their natural habitats.

Relative dominance (RD) and inversions

Prior to entering wild horse country and observing behavior there, I had based my understanding of the horse through observations of them in captivity. As I look back on it now, I can't believe the extent to which I — and many others still to this day — completely misinterpreted the species. Animals in captivity invariably do not behave at all as they do in the wild. In fact, I would go so far as to say that animals in captivity, and particularly in circuses and today's modern zoos, are wanting of anything natural. It is this clash, and the harm done by captivity, that inspired me to write *Paddock Paradise*, and now *Zoo Paradise*. While examples abound and would constitute a book in and of itself, I will give one that mirrors the bizarre "upside down" character of wild animals in captivity, including the horse. I call this an "inversion", and it goes like this . . .

In the wild, social structure of many species is based on pecking order (RD), which I've discussed earlier in this book. Pecking order — in the wild or in domestication — manifests itself as a complex spectrum of rank, for example, one horse "over the other." If there is a monarch alpha stallion, he will reign over everyone, male and female alike, in his family band. Introduce an outsider, and the pecking order invariably changes, sometimes in the strangest of ways:

$$A \text{ (monarch)} > B > C > D > E > F > G \text{ (outsider)} > A!$$

While pecking order is descendent by rank, it is also attuned to the "herd instinct." We recall, the centrifugal force that drives one horse away from another, is countered by the more powerful centripetal force that glues together the family (or species) unit. Yet, in domestication, where stallion rivalry is invariably precluded by management practices — the norm nearly everywhere — a clear departure from the "A (monarch) $> B > C > D > E > F \rightarrow$" sequence occurs. "A," facing no competition from another monarch, now "leads" the group to wherever he wants to go, typically keeping everyone behind him with the same sorts of "threats" he would wield in the wild under the pressure of stallion rivalry. Movement now takes the following formational sequence: "$F < E < D < C < B < A \text{ (monarch)} \rightarrow$". I call this shift an *inversion*.

An example of inversions: a new male horse was brought to the AANHCP Paddock Paradise and put in with our horses. Immediately, he came under assault by Apollo (our monarch alpha) who also did his best to drive his family members away from the intruder. This put Apollo and his band in rear guard formation:

$$\text{Intruder} \rightarrow A \text{ (Apollo)} > B > C > D > E > F \rightarrow$$

Two days later, the intruder deposed Apollo, precipitating a second inversion:

$$\text{Apollo} \rightarrow \text{A (Intruder)} > \text{B} > \text{C} > \text{D} > \text{E} > \text{F} \rightarrow$$

Seven days later, the intruder was returned to his owner, and the third inversion we anticipated occurred:

$$\text{F} < \text{E} < \text{D} < \text{C} < \text{B} < \text{A (Apollo)} \rightarrow$$

Because Apollo had been expelled from his normal monarch position, there was some discussion whether he would be able to resume his throne following the intruder's departure. No sooner than the exit gate of our Paddock Paradise closed behind the intruder, Apollo took a stab at him, reaching over the fence with bared teeth and pinned ears. A moment later he pushed the others away from the fence. We were left with no doubt at all!

My anticipation is that inversions will occur widely across Zoo Paradise until biologists can configure either social or territorial rivalries among its contiguous residents. "Rivalries" are central to natural selection and at the core of vitality in the wild. I believe reversing inversions is worth making the effort, but not the end of the world, as long as monarchs reign in either case.

Water holes, waterfalls, rapids and streams

Zoos, from what I've seen, typically water residents from troughs and wall-mounted watering devices that shut off flow when the animal is not drinking. Obviously, these sorts of manufactured items don't exist in the wild, and shouldn't in Zoo Paradise either. Residents should source water for drinking and bathing as they do in the wild — from water holes, springs, streams, and rivers. All of these are easily simulated in Zoo Paradise.

While some watering sources should border on being stagnant to serve some species, most can be kept "alive" through a combination of uninterrupted flow and turbulence: strong currents, whirlpools, rapids, and waterfalls, all of which add to the naturalization, beauty and vitality of Zoo Paradise. Sure also to please visitors seeking to experience the residents' natural habitats.

Diet — feeds and feeding systems

There is more to vitality than just eating the right food. How, when, and where is just as important. The specific answers lie with each species in their natural habitat, as Hediger advocated. Ungulates like the horse and zebra should be fed as we do in Paddock Paradise, but biologists will have to elucidate what will be necessary for other species. This will be a great, but worthwhile, challenge. The third pillar of NHC (for equines) specifies a "reasonably natural diet" because the actual natural diet of the wild horse has not yet been studied by qualified scientists. But my observations during my four year study of wild horse behavior (and their hooves!) suggests strongly that high de-

Wild horses and other megafauna of the late Pleistocene all faced extinction in the Western Hemisphere. My theory is that this event was precipitated by Whole Body Inflammatory Disease due to global warming and new generations of flora that were not digestible by large prey ungulates.

sert type dry forages — such as bunch grasses, legumes, and gnarly tree bark — are central to their adaptive diet. It has been suggested that some barks possess arsenic derivatives that may serve as parasiticides. Not natural (even though they are relished by horses) are the fructan-rich grass pastures we now know are laminitis traps. My theory is that new grasses fed by retreating glaciers during the late Pleistocene epoch may have been largely responsible for the horse's extinction in North America. Fructan (fructose sugar) would have attracted horses like bears to honey, and the supply was extensive. Widespread laminitis would have made *Equus ferus ferus* vulnerable to a range of large predators, including early tribes of humans in the area. Unchecked, opportunistic pathogens from the environment could have unleashed serious diseases in the wake of laminitis. I define laminitis as an inflammation of the foot's dermal structures, a symptom of Whole Body Inflammatory Disease. The latter is caused by a proliferation of aggressive bacteria and predatory viruses due to contamination of the specie's diet. Hence, climate change, unnatural diet, disease, and predation could have collectively upset the entire "food chain" in post-Pleistocene North America, leading to the extinction of many codependent species, prey and predator. My feeling is that this is a significant caveat for the planners of Zoo Paradise. Especially since the feed industry serving zoos — and domesticated livestock outside the zoos — is ladening nearly everything with sugars in one form or another. In fact, molasses and beet pulp are often the number one ingredient in equine feeds. It is no wonder that laminitis in equines has risen to epidemic levels worldwide. My personal observation of zoo ungulates is that WBID is equally present.

Life in a cell is no life at all.

Life on track is truly "paradise!"

Spirit of Zoo Paradise

The spirit of Zoo Paradise, like Paddock Paradise, beckons new directions and vistas, yet recognizes and builds upon the humanitarian wave of the Hagenbeck-Hediger Revolution. At the San Diego Zoo, Charles Schroeder's frustration and yearning to find some way to reach into the realm of vitality put him at the very gates of Zoo Paradise. The way in simply required a new paradigm with which to process the same information but in a different way so as to arrive at a new place. From the writings and advocacies of Hagenbeck, Hediger, Schroeder, and other pioneers, there are gleanable hints that they all faced a shared and scary recognition: that the whole of what they had created, regardless of the enormity of energy and resources it all took to build, regardless of the hordes of gawkers willing to pay and see, and regardless of all polished outward appearances, would somehow, in some way, have to be either rearranged completely or demolished altogether. Happily, Zoo Paradise provides a vision of vitality and a way out of their conundrum.

Attributions

Cover
- Front: Nasiroh Bt Diarto San-marta©www.123rf.com
- Back: See p. 124 credit.
- Back: See p. 120 (below) credit.

P. 2-3
- Paul Hampton©www.123rf.com

P.4
- http://commons.wikimedia.org/wiki/File:Imarriedadventure.jpg
- studiostoks©www.123rf.com

P.5
- Brenda Kean©www.123rf.com

P. 6
- https://commons.wikimedia.org/wiki/File:Giraffes_at_west_midlands_safari_park.jpg

P. 7
- Jean-Pol Grandmont — https://commons.wikimedia.org/wiki/File:0_Colosseum_-_Rome_111001_(2).JPG

P. 8
- (*Upper left*) Unknown — Public Domain. Library of Congress Reprinted - https://www.npr.org/programs/atc/features/2006/09/ota_benga/bronx_lg.jpg
- (*Bottom*) bankbuster© www.123rf.com

P. 9
- (*Left*) Public domain — https://en.wikipedia.org/wiki/File:Carl_Hagenbeck_1910_circa.jpg
- https://en.wikipedia.org/wiki/Paleo-Indians#/media/File:Glyptodon_old_drawing.jpg
- *Center/right*) Public domain — https://www.librarything.com/pic/265004

P. 10
- Public domain — https://commons.wikimedia.org/wiki/File:Safari_Park_Entrance.JPG

P.13
- United States Bureau of Land Management (BLM)

P. 14
- Unknown.

P. 15
- Jaime Jackson

P. 17
- Chadden Hunter- https://jacksonholewildlifefilmfest2017.sched.com/speaker/chadden_hunter.1wztvd4k

P. 18
- gregoryfish©www.123rf.com

P. 19
- Maria Mozgovaja©www.123rf.com

P. 25
- Jaime Jackson

P. 26
- Oleksandr Prykhodko©www.123rf.com

P. 27
- Jaime Jackson

P. 28-29
- Jill Willis

P. 30-39
- Jaime Jackson

P. 40
- Jill Willis

P. 41
- (*Above*) Jill Willis
- (*Below*) BLM

P. 42
- Jaime Jackson

P. 43
- (*Above*) BLM
- (*Below*) Jaime Jackson

P. 44
- Jaime Jackson

P. 45
- (*Above*) Luca Gandini
- (*Below*) Ben McRae©www.123rf.com

P. 46-47
- Jaime Jackson

P. 48-53
- Jill Willis

P. 54-55
- Steve Garvie — https://commons.wikimedia.org/wiki/File:Flickr_-_Rainbirder_-_High-rise_living.jpg

P. 56-57
- Jill Willis

P. 58-59
- (*Left*) Jaime Jackson
- (*Right*) Sandra Satterthwaite

P. 60-61
- Jill Willis

P. 62
- Jaime Jackson

P. 63
- (*Left*) Arno Gouw
- (*Right*) Erika Hopper

P. 64-65
- Jaime Jackson

P. 66-69
- Jill Willis

P. 70
- (*Top, middle*) Jill Willis
- (*Bottom*) Shamwari Game Reserve, South Africa

P. 71
- Mark Caldwell and Jaime Jackson

P. 72
- (*Above*) Surasak Suwanmake©www.123rf.com
- (*Below*) Jan Schneckenhaus©www.123rf.com

P. 75
- Paul Hermans — https://commons.wikimedia.org/wiki/File:Tunnelaquarium_14-05-2009_15-54-09.JPG

P. 76
- eutoch©www.123rf.com

P. 77
- Ekaterina Vidyasova©www.123rf.com

P. 79
- Jaime Jackson

P. 80
- Steffen Foerster©www.123rf.com

P. 81
- staselnik©www.123rf.com

P. 82
- Arno Gouw

P. 84
- Andrew Norris©www.123rf.com

P. 90
- Nikolai Grigoriev/Adrian Hillman/Ratko Matovic/kopecky76/Jan Stopka/Ekaterina Arkhangelskaia/macrovector/Parinya Feungchan/Irina Iarovaia/terriana/Galina Nikolaeva/Yevgenii Movliev/savanno/©www.123rf.com

P. 93
- Sina Vodjani©www.123rf.com

P. 94
- Bill Love/Blue Chameleon Ventures

P. 98
- byrdyak©www.123rf.com

P. 100
- Yahya Idiz©www.123rf.com

P. 102
- Aleksandr Stepanov©www.123rf.com

P. 118
- Mauricio Antón — https://commons.wikimedia.org/wiki/File:Ice_age_fauna_of_northern_Spain_-_Mauricio_Ant%C3%B3n.jpg

P. 120
- (*Above*) lightfieldstudios©www.123rf.com
- (*Below*) Konstantin Kalishko©www.123rf.com

P. 124
- Jill Willis

Index of Chapter Sub-headings

About the Author

I've always been a maverick thinker and doer, never satisfied with life's limits as I've perceived them to be in the mainstream. For example, after leaving the U.S. Army in early 1970 with an honorable discharge, I joined other veterans in the antiwar movement in protest of the corporate "war for profits" in Vietnam and the average American's unwitting complicity. "No business as usual" was our mantra, and on many fronts the burgeoning protest movement confronted every institution across the country. As mounting numbers of dead and wounded were returned home, the entire nation began questioning and then demanding an end to the war. In 1975 President Nixon felt the hand of the movement and shut it down — the greatest military blunder in the history of the U.S. After that, we all went own separate ways.

My calling then became "nature" and what we can learn as a species from our natural world, past and present. My books continue to tell my own story, where I've gone, what I've got myself into, with whom, and why. *Zoo Paradise* is one chapter in that story.